The Revival Styles in American Memorial Art

The Revival Styles in American Memorial Art

Peggy McDowell
and
Richard E. Meyer

Bowling Green State University Popular Press
Bowling Green, Ohio 43403

Copyright © 1994 by the Bowling Green State University Popular Press

Library of Congress Catalogue Card No: 93-72851

ISBN: 0-87972-633-4 Clothbound
      0-87972-634-2 Paperback

Cover design by Laura Darnell-Dumm

Cover photograph of Henry Augustus Coit Taylor Mausoleum, Woodlawn Cemetery, the Bronx, New York. Photo by Peggy McDowell.

CONTENTS

PREFACE

...Why call we, then, the square-built monument,
The upright column, the low-laid slab,
Tokens of death, memorials of decay?
Stand in this solemn, still assembly, man,
And learn their proper nature; for thou see'st
In these shaped stones and letter'd tables, figures
Of life...[1]

The authors of this volume, one an art historian and the other a student of folk material culture, have in their own ways and from their unique disciplinary perspectives been long fascinated with the funerary arts in America. Our own previous research and fieldwork has brought each of us to an increasing awareness of what might without exaggeration be termed a national preoccupation with the memorial arts in nineteenth century America. This period, which saw the rise of totally new concepts in the location and landscape features of cemeteries as well as radical departures from the funerary symbolism of earlier eras, would also usher in an age of dramatic, sumptuous public and private monumentation, often on a grand scale, and, as we shall see, increasingly under the dominating influence of what has come to be called the "revival styles." These movements did not originate in America: for antecedents we must look to Europe. However, it is no accident that in America they flourished with spectacular vitality, for here they found particularly fertile ground as personal and civic pride, didacticism, and the economic, political, and social climate of the times all contributed to an atmosphere which emphasized the desirability of dramatic permanent monuments to individual and societal achievement. This study is the result of our collective efforts to grapple with this most fascinating phenomenon, and it is our desire to offer the reader a degree of insight into both the influences relative to the growth of the monument industry in nineteenth century America and the dominant stylistic trends which were reflected in monument design.

The use of the word "monument" suggests many things. By the latter part of the twentieth century there are an astounding number and variety of monuments to practically every sort of thing imaginable. Designated National Monuments include natural sites, environments, and parks. Some monuments, such as dedicated auditoriums, office buildings, sun dials, water fountains, windows, fences, gates, benches, and the like, are clearly functional in nature, while others are essentially decorative. Some are architectural (a spectrum which extends from massive public structures to small private mausoleums), while others are sculptural (e.g., figures that stand on pedestals in public places and in cemeteries). In our attempt to identify and analyze the major trends in the conception and use of monuments and memorials in America, we have concentrated on those that share similar styles, forms, and functions. Although it is true that not all of those selected for review are funerary—that is, a monument related specifically to marking a grave or containing a body or bodies—they all do commemorate or perpetuate the memory of a person or persons. The major emphasis in this study is nonetheless clearly upon funerary architecture. There are in all three basic types of commemorative structures included in our analysis: public monuments that were built to honor the memory of individuals such as politically important persons; monuments that commemorate an historical event that involved great sacrifice of life, in particular battle monuments; and public and private funerary monuments such as tombs, cemetery markers, and related cenotaphs. All three types share similar stylistic

1

characteristics and reflect the immense popularity in the nineteenth and early twentieth centuries of the architecturally inspired revival styles: classical, medieval (sometimes called Gothic), and Egyptian or near Eastern.

Because our objective is to present an overview of the primary influences, trends, and designs associated with American memorial art during this period, organization by styles proved to be the most logical as a means of providing telling comparisons and analyses of types. Chronology is emphasized only when stylistic influences and questions of prototypes are important. Because the revival styles provided the basic and most consistent categorization of styles, the major emphasis is upon architectural monuments. With the exception of cemetery portals, we have excluded any monuments that have an additional, non-commemorative function, such as memorial halls, libraries, and fountains. Examples were chosen because they reveal both the variety and conformity that exists within these stylistic traditions. Some were found through fieldwork and others through a search of nineteenth-century journals and newspapers. A significant amount of the factual information in this study resulted from compiling, comparing, and evaluating materials found in popular and scholarly nineteenth century journals and newspapers as well as in archives, special collections, pamphlets, and books. Much of this primary source material is cited at the appropriate points in the notes that accompany the text of this volume. Other secondary and corollary sources are indicated in the notes and in the bibliography.

The topic of American memorial art is vast and diversified, as clearly evidenced by the number of excellent critical studies which have appeared in recent years. Even within the more limited focus of this particular work, we are certainly aware that our research has by no means exhausted the subject, and the numerous illustrations and textual discussions found in this book may perhaps best be viewed as representative examples. We would be more than pleased if what we present here provides an inspiration and starting point for future scholarship and, perhaps most importantly of all, preservation of this unique and fascinating aspect of American culture.

PART I

The Rise of Memorial Art in America

Tombs, monuments, and markers created to commemorate the dead have always been sources of inspiration for the arts of western cultures.[2] Many civilizations have in fact been analyzed and evaluated primarily through examination of their funerary arts. Tomb decorations and furnishings reveal, amongst other things, deep-seated religious beliefs, ontological theories, and cultural self-esteem. Funerary arts, which often have been preserved when all else has decayed, not only disclose religious and other cultural preoccupations but also reveal a stubborn resistance of humankind to sink into oblivion. However humble or grand, these monuments emphatically insist "I existed" in the face of an otherwise evolving, changing world.

Interest in commemorative monuments and related imagery has varied from period to period and culture to culture, in each case leaving a rich and sometimes mysterious legacy of material artifacts for succeeding generations to admire and ponder. The Egyptians were engrossed in funerary art production encompassing a variety of evocative forms. Greeks are forever frozen on their geometric funerary vases and classical marble sarcophagi. The Etruscans created an optimistic duplication of their homes and pleasures—feasting, singing, dancing, and loving in their necropolises. The Romans carried the art of funerary architecture, ornamentation, and sculpture to extremes of sumptuousness, and emphasized as well other, non-funerary commemorative monuments in their culture. Christians enshrined the bodies of saints, and important parishioners were buried in diverse types of monuments within the churches. From the medieval period through the eighteenth century, most of the architecturally and sculpturally significant monuments in western culture were reserved for the nobility of church and state. In the nineteenth century, however, with the advent of radical social and political reform and the concomitant rise of the individual and individuality, there was an increase of interest in commemorative arts amongst all levels of society, regardless of religious conviction or family lineage. Writing in 1820, architect John Mills would sum up the common purposes of funerary monumentation as follows:

To cherish the recollection of those who have lived an ornament and benefit to the world, or a delight to their immediate connexions [sic], is not only a duty we owe to their memory, but an advantage to ourselves.... Clinging to their remains, we follow them to the grave, and... we wish to perpetuate these feelings of admiration and affection, by some lasting momento of their worth. For this purpose, the funeral monument has been invented, as the most appropriate and durable method of recording our sentiments.... It perpetuates the name and virtues of the deceased, it fills the bosom of the living with generous and noble sentiments....[3]

In nineteenth century America, many of these commemorative monuments were located in cemeteries; others, not specifically funerary, were erected in conspicuous places within towns and cities or in parks. These monuments shared the common objective of perpetuating the memory or the ideals of family members, local or national heroes, or other culturally important individuals. Historical markers also helped remind citizens of battles won or lost and indicated sites of particular educational importance. Amidst the commercial clutter and acceleration of the late twentieth century, these public monuments regrettably often go unnoticed and unattended.

This expanded popular interest in the commemorative arts stemmed from a variety of motivations and interests, the majority of which reflect significant social and economic changes in the West, particularly within the countries of France, Great Britain, and the United States. The nineteenth century is often equated with the Victorian era, a conceptual period which implies the cultures linked with Great Britain during the reign of Queen Victoria (1837-1901). However, the countries directly experiencing the surging interest in the commemorative arts did not find this interest restricted by such arbitrary concepts as Victorian temporal or geographical boundaries. The Western cultures shared a common architectural vocabulary in the nineteenth century, a vocabulary of forms and types that derived its energy from the revival of stylistic features associated with previous periods in Western history or, in some instances, with the recent rediscovery of non-Western cultures. The revival styles, especially the classical, Gothic, and Egyptian, dominated nineteenth century architecture and were particularly adaptable and applicable to the commemorative arts.

Prompted by industrial and political revolutions in Europe and America near the close of the eighteenth century, the lower and middle classes, ignored socially and politically but a few decades before, steadily gained power and influence as the new century progressed. With the ever growing influence of the middle class in particular came a *nouveau riche* interest in material manifestations of one's status and family heritage. This materialism would become especially evident in funeral panoply and rituals, where, amongst its several manifestations, it fostered the desire on the part of many people to build ever more impressive mausoleums, tombs, and cemetery monuments rather than continue to be content with erecting the simpler and more traditional tombstone or slab. This latter phenomenon—that is, the appearance of a numerous variety of rather ostentatious private monuments to ordinary individuals—was further prompted by a political and philosophical climate that emphasized the innate worth of the individual, a climate, one might argue, that was actively encouraged by new democratic governments in Europe as well as in America and by attitudes born out of late eighteenth and early nineteenth century concepts associated with Romanticism.

The elevation of other, non-funerary, civic monuments was especially prompted by political and sentimental influences, a phenomenon which had striking consequences in the United States. The new country, known already for its social and cultural opportunities, had realized a more stable society after the turbulent years of the American Revolution. The Ten Amendments (i.e., the Bill of Rights) ratified in late 1791 guaranteed freedoms that further reinforced popular support of the Constitution and the new American government. With their newly earned independence from foreign controls, Americans projected optimism and pride in their identity. The years of settlement and revolution had provided a wealth of legitimate heroes worthy of tangible symbols that reflected the citizens' esteem and respect, and monuments would help to fill this need for recognition and commemoration. Precedents were not hard to find. Statues of old-world nobility and folk heroes ornamented the gardens, parks, and avenues of all major European cities, just as impressive tombs filled the walls along the aisles of major European cathedrals and parish churches. On this side of the Atlantic, attitudes of pride and respect for heroic individuals who reflected the values and set the standards of American politics and philosophies encouraged the construction of a wealth of publicly sponsored commemorative civic monuments and statuary, as well as publicly sponsored tombs.

Some specific examples of attitudes about American heroes can perhaps best be demonstrated by elements of anecdotal information concerning Washington's tomb at Mount Vernon. Of all the figures in American history, George Washington has been most often commemorated, and the "cult of Washington" that developed during the nineteenth century expressed a sentiment bordering on religious veneration for the father of the American Republic.

Washington had requested in his will that a new family vault be constructed on the grounds of Mount Vernon, his family estate located sixteen miles south of the present-day District of Columbia. The old vault, too small and in need of repair, was unfortunately located on a hillside that suffered damage from erosion. However, until the new crypt was ultimately constructed in 1831, Washington's body would lie with the remains of his family in the old vault. The delay of some forty years from the president's death to the building of the new vault was the result of several factors. Soon after Washington's death in 1791, Congress had moved to build a funerary monument to the first president within the newly formed District of Columbia. The legislators suggested that Washington's body be placed in a temporary crypt under the dome of the Capitol Building until his monument was completed. This plan was never realized as proposed, however, and a descendant finally made the determination that Washington's own stated desire to be buried in a new family vault at Mount Vernon should be respected. In the meantime, the old vault had been violated when an intruder, somewhat in the vein of a medieval relic hunter, had attempted to steal Washington's remains. This event, probably as much as anything, encouraged the decision to finally construct a sturdy new vault.

This protracted and somewhat bizarre history of Washington's tomb was colorfully reported some years hence in an article in *Harper's New Monthly Magazine*, which typified in many respects nineteenth century attitudes towards Washington and other American cultural heroes. The author, a recent visitor to Mount Vernon, adopted an eloquently moralistic tone when he reproved the presence of a daguerreotypist situated near the tomb to take pictures of visitors to the site:

Oh, how every sentiment of respect and reverence for the illustrious dead—every emotion born of a true American spirit—rose up in severe rebuke of this disgraceful traffic in the vestibule of that temple wherein the good and true of all nations would delight to pour their origins! I thought of a scene in old Jerusalem, when, in another temple, the tables of the 'money changers and the seats of those who sold doves' were overturned.[4]

Of particular interest to the readers of the *Harper's* article might well have been the description, replete with the gruesome concern for detail typical of certain strains of Romantic literature, of the opening of the crypt in 1837 to transfer the bodies of George and Martha Washington to new marble sarcophagi. These stone coffins, presented by John Struthers of Philadelphia, are located in the tomb vestibule. The story of the sarcophagi, along with the roles played by Struthers and William

Strickland, also of Philadelphia, is reported in a brief publication of 1840 entitled *The Tomb of Washington at Mount Vernon*. Its author was Strickland, a prominent architect and engineer responsible for the design of numerous private and public buildings including the United States Mints in Philadelphia, New Orleans, and Charlotte, North Carolina. Perhaps most importantly in the immediate context, he was also an active designer of monuments. Struthers, a builder and marble mason, had frequently collaborated with Strickland, and he or his firm was responsible for a number of the impressive monuments located in Philadelphia's famous Laurel Hill Cemetery. Much like the author of the *Harper's* article, Strickland in *The Tomb of Washington* continuously uses religious terminology when referring to Washington and the "hallowed spot" where he lies buried. Both sarcophagi in the crypt are simple: Martha Washington's is entirely without decoration, and the lid of the president's, designed by Strickland, bears the family coat of arms (see Fig. 1). The execution of the design was by a member of Struther's firm, John Hill.[5]

Struthers, Strickland, and descendants of George and Martha Washington were present when the bodies were transferred and permanently sealed within the sarcophagi. The location of the remains in the front of the tomb was well planned because it allows for visitors to view the sarcophagi through the iron gate of the vaulted vestibule. A rear burial chamber is underground within a hill of earth. Around the exterior are various obelisk markers for family members buried within the crypt. The site was frequently reproduced in nineteenth century publications and souvenir lithographs (see, for example, Fig. 2). Mount Vernon was ultimately purchased by a patriotic group of women who formed the Mount Vernon Ladies' Association of the Union in 1858. Money for the purchase was raised by public subscription, its appeal couched in the sentimental language of the nineteenth century deemed most appropriate when speaking of national heroes:

The Lid

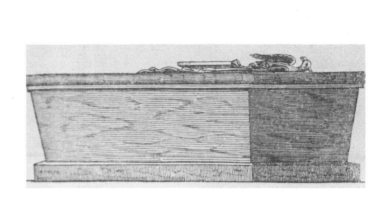

Fig. 1. Sarcophagus of George Washington, as illustrated in *Harper's New Monthly Magazine* (1859).

The object of the Mount Vernon Ladies' Association shall be: 'To perpetuate the sacred memory of "The Father of his Country" and, with loving hands, to guard and protect the hallowed spot where rest his mortal remains.'[6]

Along with the leaders of the Revolutionary War and the new American Congress, heroes of the War of 1812 and of the Civil War provided further impetus for public commemoration in the nineteenth century. The Civil War had a particularly strong influence on the lives and hearts of people from both the North and South. Not only leaders, but also common soldiers, merited recognition for their heroism and sacrifice. Emotionalism ran high. James Russell Lowell, in his "Ode Recited at the Harvard Commemoration, July 21, 1865," reflects some of the intense feelings of the age. The lengthy poem, first read to commemorate those from Harvard who had fought and died in the Civil War, includes the following sentiment:

> In these brave ranks I only see the gaps,
> Thinking of the dear ones whom the dumb turf wraps,

> Dark to the triumph which they died to gain:
> Fitlier may others greet the living,
> For me the past is unforgiving;
> I with uncovered head
> Salute the sacred dead,
> Who went, and who return not....'[7]

Inspired by a sense of moral responsibility and didacticism, many communities collectively sponsored the erection of markers to soldiers and sailors who had fought and died in service to their cause. Although these monuments did not always mark gravesites, they often took on the symbolism of a funerary marker. Usually a local monument society controlled the design selection, the funding and the building of the monument. Various activities and entertainments were held to raise monies, and an emotional appeal was usually made to the public through the press and speeches. Most people had been touched by the war, and the financing of these commemorative monuments became both labors of love and moral commitments. The unveiling ceremonies of the finished creations were grand social events that included parades and rousing speeches. Along with military monuments conspicuously located

Fig. 2. Nineteenth century lithographic print of the tomb of George Washington.

within towns and cities, other testimonials were erected on battlefields and in cemeteries.[8] Many national cemeteries were established as a result of the Civil War. The land on which the soldiers fought and died and in which they were interred became sanctified by sacrifice. The sentiments of a nation were aptly summarized in words from President Abraham Lincoln's 1863 "Address at the Dedication of the Gettysburg National Cemetery":

We have met on a great battlefield of that war. We have come to dedicate a portion of that field as a final resting-place for those who here gave their lives that this nation might live. It is altogether fitting and proper that we should do this.

But, in a larger sense, we cannot dedicate—we cannot consecrate—we cannot hallow—this ground. The brave men, living, and dead, who struggled here have consecrated it, far above our poor power to add or detract.[9]

Still, survivors from both sides of the conflict did indeed dedicate, consecrate, and hallow the burial grounds which held their beloved dead. And the feelings were no less intense for those who failed to achieve victory as a result of their sacrifices, as may be seen in a poem by Henry Timrod entitled "Ode Sung at the Occasion of Decorating the Graves of the Confederate Dead at Magnolia Cemetery, Charleston, S.C., June 16, 1866," which appeared in the *Charleston Courier* on June 18, 1866:

Sleep sweetly in your humble graves,
   Sleep, martyrs of a fallen cause;
Though yet no marble column craves
   The pilgrim here to pause.
Stoop, angels, hither from the skies!
   There is no holier spot of ground
Than where defeated valor lies,
   By mourning beauty crowned!

National and religious holidays provided special motivations for decorating the graves of the brave dead, and popular journals of the period frequently illustrated figures placing flowers atop the graves of those who had perished in the Civil War.

In the national and private cemeteries where soldiers were interred, simple markers often indicated individual graves, and a larger monument was collectively shared by all. Like those constructed in city squares and parks, these military monuments erected in the cemeteries became predictable in their iconography and features (see Fig. 3). In the well-established tradition of industry and commercialism, many monument manufacturers specialized in military monuments and sent salesmen through northern and southern cities to sell their goods, which often consisted of stock patterns reproduced in large quantities. A spirit of competitiveness, not infrequently encouraged by monument salesmen who were prone to exploit private and civic sentiments, often arose between communities as one city strove to make its expression of patriotism equal to or greater than that of another city. Indeed, so many military monuments were built during the years following the Civil War that the previously cited stylistic eclecticism and monotonous redundancy became embarrassing problems. In certain instances, those artists who were in fact creating original work felt it necessary to take out patents to discourage imitators from using their designs without proper credit.

In addition to public interest generated by the emergence of home grown American heroes and the desire to commemorate the dead of several wars, popular journalism in the nineteenth century helped spread an awareness of monument types and also helped make memorial structures more fashionable and popular. Architectural journals and bulletins[10] kept the art public informed about contemporary monuments by the inclusion of descriptive sections on the topic. General readers learned of these matters through articles in popular magazines which frequently illustrated or described commemorative structures built in American and foreign cities. The frequent printing of information of this nature is but one evidence of the enormous interest displayed by nineteenth century Americans towards matters of commemoration, particularly those linked to a funerary context. Although human mortality remains a reality no matter

Fig. 3. Typical Civil War cemetery monument. City View Cemetery, Salem, Oregon. Photo by Richard E. Meyer.

Certainly there were ample reasons for the constant reminders about death. The nineteenth century American population suffered from epidemics, warfare, and other factors contributing to exceedingly high mortality rates. An element of pervasive melancholy suffused the popular literature of the age, both reflecting and perpetuating this mood. Sentimental poetry dealing with death was regularly published in newspapers and magazines. These popular and frequently maudlin poems, while possessing little if any lierary merit, reflected a preoccupation with romantic attitudes toward death remarkably similar to that of the late eighteenth century English graveyard school of poets:

> In the little churchyard yonder,
> > Buried are the treasures dear,
> In the starry land above us
> > Swell the ones I love most dear
> There's my home affection centers
> > Where the loved and loving meet
> Earth no other home can give me,
> > None I'll have till there we meet.[11]

> * * * * * * * *

> There's a city vast yet voiceless,
> > growing ever street on street
> Whither friends with friend e'er meeting,
> > ever meeting never greet;
> And where rivals fierce and vengeful calm,
> > and silent mutely meet:
> > never greeting ever meet.

what the time period or culture, the nineteenth century in America was a period in which death was grandiosely ritualized and sentimentalized. Religion obviously played a part in encouraging the panoply that surrounded death and commemoration; however, inducement came also from a conforming social hierarchy at times seemingly obsessed with concerns of prestige and status. Sentimentalizing blended with historicizing to make the funerary and related commemorative arts a high priority in the value scale of Americans.

Hushed are all these mansions,
    barred and bolted door and gate;
Narrow all the walls and earthy,
    and the roof-trees steep and straight.
Room for all!—the high and lowly
    Rich and poor have equal mate.
    Equal dwell and equal mate.
Beckons ever this mute city
    to its comrade living gay;
To its comrade laughing loudly,
    sitting on the pulsing bay;
Drawing from its masqueraders pale,
    white spectres day by day:
    Spectres now, men yesterday.[12]
      * * * * * * * *
How great unto the living seem the dead!
How sacred, solemn; how heroic grown!
How vast and vague, as they obscurely tread
The shadowy confines of the dim unknown—
For they have met the monster that we dread,
Have learned the secret not to mortal
shown....[13]

Nor was the emphasis verbal alone: sentimental visual imagery featuring cemetery scenes and grieving family members was a regular feature in popularly read newspapers and magazines. Readers were thus constantly reminded of the inevitability of death; and, by the same token, one may conclude that these publications voiced popular opinions and reflected common interests of the period.[14]

One of the poems cited above, "The Living and the Dead," which was printed in *Frank Leslie's Illustrated Newspaper* in 1865, reveals in its opening line—"How great unto the living seem the dead!"—an attitude particularly prevalent during this period. In the latter part of the eighteenth century, death, with increasing frequency, stimulated society to fantasize, romanticize, and question. This philosophical and emotional involvement with death would continue and remain pervasive throughout the greater part of the nineteenth century. Scientific and medical discoveries, as well as religious questionings, caused more insecurity. "Can these dry bones live again?" was a voiced question, or at least a subliminal worry. By extending funerary and mourning rituals, the living prolonged psychological contact with the

"dear departed" and thus resisted obliterating the presence, at least symbolically or emotionally, of the deceased. Moreover, these same rituals would await the survivors when it became their time to die. Social mores thus encouraged a continuation of these practices: general acceptance of the rituals assured the living that they, too, would not be easily forgotten. Funeral monuments and markers were a further means of perpetuating contact between the mortal and immortal realms. Perhaps, too, there was another motivation that subconsciously persisted, one grounded in a belief still widely accepted in many non-Western cultures, the notion that the spirit of the deceased could somehow prove useful or harmful to the living. For any number of reasons, therefore, proper homage to the departed helped to assure a desired harmony between the living and the dead. The panoply of death was a vitally important part of this ritual.

The rituals and symbols of death were extensive and persisted well beyond the time of the burial. In most areas of the country, it was common for funeral memorabilia to be collected and prominently displayed in the home. Funerary photographs were taken for the family portrait album and for display. Death notices were framed and draped in black crepe to be placed on the parlour table; often they were folded and preserved in the family Bible. It was not unusual for a family member to create figurative memorial records for home display; these were somewhat predictable in their iconography of urns, willows, altars, churches, and mourning figures. Although frequently rendered in inks and paints, embroidered and cross-stitched memorials were often produced as well. Commemorative lithographs were also available for recording dates of the deceased when a more colorful and professional print was desired for home decor (see Fig. 4).[15] Hair of the deceased was collected and fashioned into jewelry for grieving loved ones. A very personal, perhaps even fetishistic material, hair was also used to create figurative immortelles framed behind glass. Details of these hair designs varied from wreaths and floral themes to traditional funerary motifs, and they were

Fig. 4. Nineteenth century commemorative lithograph.

displayed in the family parlour as a constant and intimate reminder of the departed dead.[16]

Along with these domestic manifestations of the growing cult of mourning, two practical influences also contributed extensively to the rise of the commemorative arts in the United States. These were, on the one hand, the widespread establishment and enormous public acceptance of regional, non-sectarian cemeteries based upon popular European models, and its equally important corollary, the dramatic growth and transformation of the quarry and monument industries.

The concept of major regional cemeteries saw its origins in Europe, where Paris proved the leader in this endeavor. For several hundreds of years prior to the late eighteenth century, Parisians had buried their dead in the consecrated ground surrounding the urban churches. As a consequence, these cemeteries eventually became not only vastly overcrowded but particularly unaesthetic as well. The then popular theory that miasmas arising from burial grounds produced epidemics was undoubtedly reinforced by the dreadful odors that came from within these ossuary yards. These same theories holding that cemeteries were the sources of illness were also frequently expressed in nineteenth century American publications.[17] In the late eighteenth century, when Paris's *Cimetière des Innocents* simply could not accommodate more bodies, the French municipality finally moved to forbid any future burial in urban churchyards. The old cemeteries were eventually replaced by several metropolitan cemeteries. Père Lachaise, or the Eastern Cemetery, consecrated in December, 1804, was the first and largest of these. It did not take much persuasion, it seems, to convince people to bury their dead away from the precincts of the churchyards. The spacious landscape and greenery of Père Lachaise and its counterparts were inviting indeed when compared to the crowded, putrescent state of the city churchyards.[18]

The idea of municipal cemeteries was particularly well timed, for the growing urban society was putting increasing population pressures upon the already crowded cities. The spacious lands of the new cemetery grounds provided city dwellers with an Elysian garden environment for their eternal sleep. The plots were usually sold in perpetuity, an assurance welcomed in otherwise changing times. The bones would not be moved after a certain period to ossuary chambers, as was the standard practice in the more crowded urban cemeteries. Furthermore, the environment within the walls of the "rural" metropolitan cemeteries offered persons of all backgrounds and levels in society the opportunity, funds permitting, to create for themselves the idealistic final dwelling place. The art in these cemeteries reflects the dominant values and tastes of the period. And even for those who could afford only the simplest marker, the metropolitan cemetery, such as Père Lachaise, at least provided fashionable surroundings supplied by wealthier neighbors and the beauty of nature. Gardens had become increasingly precious environments, contrasting with the congestion and suppression of greenspaces in cities, and the "gardens of the dead" represented by these new cemeteries at times fulfilled roles other than their strictly utilitarian ones.[19]

London followed the example set by Paris, and a General Cemetery Company was incorporated in 1830 to investigate and establish, in the words of the title page of the *Prospectus of the General Cemetery Company*, "places of interment, secure from violation, inoffensive to public health and decency, and ornamental to the metropolis." In the *Prospectus*, the founding members emphasized the limited local burial grounds and the unwholesome practice of burying the dead in churches. Continued churchyard burials had proven infeasible, and in some areas was actually forbidden by law. One contributor to the *Prospectus* wrote a grandiose description of Père Lachaise to convince readers of the desirability of such a "scene, as it were, of enchantment," where "...within a space of sixty-four acres, [we] learn that the remains of 100,000 mortals are here consigned to the tomb.... No small portion were endowed with worldly goods, and their families or friends have erected to them 15,000 monuments.... The prince and the peasant are, nevertheless, equal here."[20] The goal of the company, so the *Prospectus* claims, was to provide a comparable cemetery for metropolitan London. After systematic study of ground plans and architectural competitions for layout, chapels, and gates, Kensal Green Cemetery was officially opened to receive its first burial in 1833, and its social and financial success soon encouraged the establishment of other London regional cemeteries. The South Metropolitan Cemetery at Norwood was opened in 1837, followed by Highgate Cemetery in 1839.[21]

The decade of 1830-40 was also an active period for the establishment of metropolitan (often termed "rural," a term descriptive of both their contemporary locations with reference to the core cities that they served and their desired aesthetic) cemeteries in the United States. Mount Auburn Cemetery in Cambridge, Massachusetts, was founded in 1831 to serve the population of the greater Boston area. Philadelphia's Laurel Hill Cemetery followed in 1836, and fashionable Green-Wood Cemetery in 1839 in Brooklyn to accommodate the needs of New York City area residents, with the dedication of Baltimore's Green Mount Cemetery occurring that same year. Other cities followed suit as needs demanded, to the degree that by the 1860s there were more than sixty of these new rural cemeteries operating in various parts of the United States.[22] The cemeteries became a retreat for the living. Family and friends visited the graves of their loved ones, while other visitors used the grounds for outings. Proper etiquette and behavior were required and regulations were often published in guide books. Both Laurel Hill and Green-Wood, for instance, restricted admission of any unaccompanied children. Food or refreshments were not allowed, nor were dogs. At Green-Wood a special ticket of admission was required unless the visitor owned cemetery property, and any person disturbing the peaceful nature of the grounds by noise or improper conduct was subject to expulsion. Tour books provided information for the more inquisitive visitor. Routes were suggested, with data provided

about the monuments along the way. In the late nineteenth century a carriage tour was available at Green-Wood for a nominal fee of twenty-five cents, and souvenir booklets were sold to visitors.[23]

The increased number and expanded role of cemeteries in nineteenth century America served to encourage the rapid development of allied, and sometimes entirely new industries and professions, among them cemetery horticulture and planning and the fabrication and marketing of increasingly more elaborate monuments. The dramatic growth of the monument trade in the United States was spurred by the expanding quarry industry and the coming-of-age of American-born sculptors and craftsmen.[24] Americans no longer had to depend on European quarries and technicians to fabricate their work, although some designers still insisted upon European fabricators for sculptural duplication. The granite industries in particular flourished in the eastern United States, producing fine quality stone that weathered extremely well.[25] The monument trade, whether specializing in granite, marble, or, near the end of the century, white bronze (zinc), was to become quite lucrative and provided numerous jobs for laborers, skilled craftsmen, and artists.

With rising demands came mass production and its inevitable corollary, mundane repetition, especially of the less costly designs. The taste and quality of many of these monuments are questionable even by the generous standards of the nineteenth century. And while many well-known sculptors and architects would undertake commissioned cemetery work for their clients, the majority of monuments were designed and fashioned by artisans who limited their talents to gravestone production alone. Unhappily, these craftsmen most frequently resorted to using the same limited repertory of styles and types in stock duplications and stock patterns which shallowly reflected changing fads and fashions. An article entitled "Fashions in Gravestones," published in the June, 1885 issue of *The Granite-Cutter's Journal*, observed the arbitrary rise and fall in popularity of gravemarker types and styles and compared the fluctuating preferences in tombstones to similar changing fads in ladies' hats! Be that as it may, it seems evident that a large percentage of monument dealers and their customers were quite satisfied with basic functional designs and were not overly disturbed by the fact that these monuments duplicated others in monotonously redundant fashion. Stock designs were readily available, far less expensive, and apparently considered to be at least adequately fashionable. For those who desired and could afford a greater range of choices, creative variations (relatively speaking) were available, or special designs could be commissioned.

It was, of course, usually the wealthier client who had the option and whose monuments distinguish themselves among the less individualized stock patterns, and it followed that the more fashionable cemeteries generally boasted the larger number of individualized designs. Naturally enough, the wealthy often chose to be buried near the wealthy, and metropolitan cemetery planning was frequently arranged to accommodate these elite families of American society. And it is surely no surprise that the more personalized, unique designs which grace these fashionable sections (see Fig. 5) should prove far more interesting than those dictated by mass production. These individualized monuments reveal personal choices and tastes and are also the products of upper-middle or upper-class patronage. Because many such funerary monuments, and especially large family mausoleums, took a significant amount of time to build, the designs were often selected and the tombs built quite some time before they were actually needed. This further reassured the wealthy owners not only that a fitting environment would house their bodies upon their deaths but, perhaps even more importantly, that a permanent reminder of their economic power and social standing would remain on site to be admired by generations as yet unborn.

Fig. 5. Unique, personalized Victorian-era gravemarker. George S. Bangs monument (1877), Rosehill Cemetery, Chicago. Photo by Norma Eid.

PART II

The Revival Styles
and American Memorial Art

1. INTRODUCTION

Despite the redundancy of stock designs, especially in less expensive models, varieties of scale, style, sculptural detail, and artistic creativity do definitely appear, and indeed, in the final analysis, may be said to ultimately define the distinctiveness of nineteenth century American funerary monuments. Many prestigious metropolitan and rural cemeteries have preserved in microcosm an expression of an ideal environment and vividly illustrate cross-cultural examples of the most sought after tastes and styles of the times. The revival styles dominate the period, and imaginative, unpredictable applications of eclectic elements are everywhere displayed. The charm of variety and the unabashed fantasies of revival design often make these cemeteries spectacular outdoor museums for students of period architecture, sculpture, and the decorative arts in general. While it is neither the intent nor the purpose of the present study to engage in a lengthy discussion or definition of the Romantic attitude which permeated the art worlds of Europe and America in the nineteenth century, the underlying importance of this sweeping movement in the arts cannot be overlooked. One facet of this importance, particularly relevant to our purposes here, has been aptly summarized by architectural historian Wayne Andrews: the Romantic architects, he notes, "aimed—if we may hazard a guess as to the collective dream of a generation—at introducing into architecture the fourth dimension, time itself, and their Grecian, Gothic, Italian, Egyptian and other fantasies are best remembered as so many invitations to explore the poetry of time."[26] Cemetery and other nineteenth century memorial designs dramatically illustrate this potential of the revival styles to capture and perpetuate time through the use of motifs inspired by the past to immortalize contemporary individuals and to preserve their memory for future generations.

There were actually many reasons why for a growing faction of American society the revival style designs were preferred over the traditional, often nondistinctive, slabs and other markers which had characterized funerary monumentation up until this point. Influences are varied: however, one particularly important stimulus extends back to eighteenth century Europe, a period which saw an increased awareness of and interest in ancient tombs and funerary artifacts resulting from recent publications on archaeological sites. Many design elements in nineteenth century funerary art were in fact prefigured in Giovanni Battista Piranesi's popular eighteenth century prints, an influence the full extent of which has never been fully appreciated. Although Piranesi was also an architect, he is undoubtedly best known for his prints, and most of his professional career was spent in Rome, where views of the contemporary buildings and ancient ruins served as an inspiration for various series of plates. Tombs were of particular interest to him. Among his earliest studies in Rome, published as *Prima Parte di Architetture e Prospettive* in 1743, Piranesi included views of imaginary Roman buildings, ruins of tombs and sarcophagi, and a hypothetical reconstruction of a Roman emperor's mausoleum. In 1754, he began his *Le Antichità Romane*, which was later expanded to four volumes. Two of these, Volumes II and III, are of particular interest here, as they are exclusively concerned with views of tombs and funerary monuments. The discovery and exploitation of tomb artifacts still frequently occurred in eighteenth century Italy, and scenes such as the tombs along the Appian Way allowed Piranesi the opportunity to combine antiquarian documentation with nostalgic romanticism and imaginative fantasizing.

The lore and love of ruins, further enhanced by the excavations of Pompeii and Herculaneum, were international manifestations of Rococo temperaments. Travel on the "grand tour" commonly included visits to ancient Roman ruins and historical sites. The learned aristocracy of Europe, after studying the works of Vitruvius and Palladio, combined education with pleasure in these tours, which occasionally included visits to Egypt, Greece, and Turkey along with the traditional cities of the continent. Descriptions of ruins were frequently documented in letters and inscribed in travel journals. Piranesi's prints were collected by traveling gentility, and the artist eventually accumulated a following of artists, semi-scholars, and collectors from throughout Europe. The British in particular seem to have felt a strong affinity for Piranesi's illustrations, and most family libraries of any consequence included original editions or reprints of his work. The charm and consequent popularity of his prints in the eighteenth and nineteenth centuries rests in the fact that his illustrations were not pedagogical anthologies of antiquities, but rather creative interpretations of the rustic, unmanicured conditions of ancient ruins and reconstructions seen through the eyes of a dramatic and inventive creator. His documentation of Roman buildings, such as those seen in the *Vendute di Roma* series, is ultimately overshadowed by the fanciful and independent inventiveness found in his *Parere su I' Architettura*, the *Carceri* series, and the designs published in *Diverse Maniere*.

Ironically, when the later half of the eighteenth century saw the end of the Rococo, with the consequent revival of classical art in France and the birth of Romanticism in England, Piranesi's work may have had appeal to both the neoclassical advocates and the romantics, though his influence was probably greatest among the European romantic artists as classicism blended with romanticism in the early nineteenth century. Except for the more prosperous architects who could afford travel, many builders and designers in the late eighteenth and nineteenth centuries had limited exposure to original antique works, and it was only through collections of illustrations that these artisans could learn and compare sculpture and architecture from different times and countries. This would have been especially true of American artists and craftsmen. Given these circumstances, it seems certain that Piranesi would have been generously studied and admired by students of the antique in America and abroad. With creative eclecticism, the printmaker imaginatively combined monu-

ments of Roman, Greek, Etruscan, and Egyptian types, and it is these same types, along with Gothic revival styles, which appear in tomb designs at Père Lachaise and comparable cemeteries. Although Piranesi's illustrations were not as acceptable to pedants as more academic studies, his works were without question extraordinarily influential on the popular level.

Also influential were architectural reference books which were published for scholars, students, and connoisseurs. These conventional sources often encouraged a common language of styles and forms, and this vocabulary of design types and styles, which defies regionalism, made a considerable and lasting impact upon funerary design. Through influences such as these, and for reasons driven by a renewed interest in antiquity and new philosophical underpinnings of taste and style, the revival styles, fundamentally international in scope, were especially exploited in cemetery and related commemorative designs in Europe and America.

Before proceeding to an in-depth examination of the revival styles, it is important to emphasize that the basic types of cemetery markers ordinarily used in early America prior to the revival period would also continue in popularity throughout the nineteenth century. Three types in particular, all traditional to Europe, dominated early American graveyards: the tombstone, or tablet; the horizontal slab; and the table box, or bench tomb. A print from an 1871 *Harper's New Monthly Magazine* of the Cooper Burying Ground in Cooperstown, New York (Fig. 6) illustrates all three of these basic types.[27] Certainly the most traditional and universal of these is the tombstone, a form that can be traced back to the ancient funerary stele. On-site studies of early American tombstones can best be made in the colonial states, where an abundance of early graveyards are preserved, often in excellent condition. The motifs and inscriptions on these vertical slabs were most generally produced by local folk artists, and the most frequently repeated motifs that ornamented the tops of the gravestones were skulls, often with wings (Fig. 7), other mortality emblems such as hour-

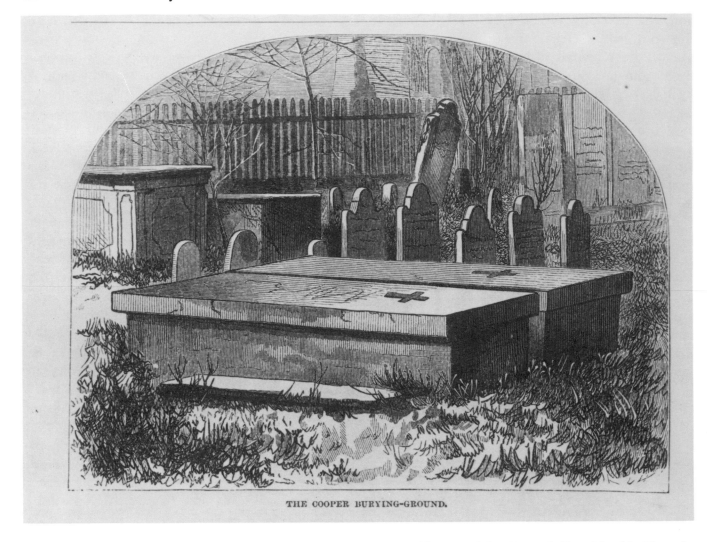

THE COOPER BURYING-GROUND.

Fig. 6. Cooper Burying Ground, Cooperstown, New York, as illustrated in *Harper's New Monthly Magazine* (1871).

glasses and coffins, cherub-type faces, also with wings, geometrical or floret wheels, urns, and willow trees.[28] Of all the motifs which dominated seventeenth and eighteenth century tombstone designs in America, perhaps the most striking and memorable are those which display gruesomely blatant images of death and decay.

A second early means of marking graves that continued to be used in the nineteenth century is a rectangular slab of stone placed horizontally on top of the grave and level with or slightly above the ground. Bricks or stone usually support the slab and line a portion of the grave. The third type of marker is similar to this, but instead of the slab being low or level with the ground it is elevated to a noticeable degree above the grave. The slab could be raised simply by extending the supporting level of bricks or stone, with the height varying from a few courses to the point where it results in a full scale table-like rectangular box. This form in particular offered the potential for a great deal of variety in structural decoration, including motifs inspired by the ancient sarcophagus as well as period designs found on church altars, tables, chests and boxes. An ornate example of this type is illustrated by the monument to an early Virginia governor, Edward Nott (Fig. 8), which was imported from England in the eighteenth century and erected upon its present site in Bruton Parish Churchyard, Williamsburg, Virginia.[29] Throughout this period, despite the gradual emergence of certain distinctively American forms in the commemorative arts, there

Fig. 7. Winged skull gravestone typical of Puritan period. Phipps Street Burial Ground, Charlestown, Massachusetts. Photo by Daniel and Jessie Lie Farber.

Fig. 8. Edward Nott monument, Bruton Parish Churchyard, Williamsburg, Virginia. Photo by Peggy McDowell.

remained as well a continuing interchange between Europe and America which helped foster the international flavor of funerary art styles and designs.

2. CLASSICAL REVIVAL

The classical revival is broadly identified by a variety of features borrowed from diverse periods and cultures. Major classical revival sources include antique Roman and Greek prototypes as well as Renaissance, Palladian, or academic interpretations of the antique and eclectic combinations of all of these. In the eighteenth century, American architects and builders, like their European counterparts and in keeping with their educations, reacted against the ornate Baroque and lavish Rococo styles and revived a classicism inspired by the principles of Andrea Palladio. The resulting dominant style in the early Federal period which followed the American Revolution was Georgian. Georgian Palladianism was eventually modified or superseded by another form of classicism inspired by the Roman revival. During the French Empire period, Napoleon identified his rule with the imperial phases of Roman civilization. American theorists like Thomas Jefferson, on the other hand, related philosophically to the republican aspects of ancient Rome. Jefferson, who was an exceptionally well-rounded man with both political and artistic skills, did a great deal to sanction the official acceptance of Roman revival styles in early America. Actually, both the Roman and Greek revival styles were admired during this period. The ancient Greeks were respected for their philosophical, literary, and artistic contributions to western civilization, and the arts of this culture were interpreted as a reflection of rationality, perfection, and beauty. By association, then, any style that professed allegiance to the intellectual and aesthetic character of the ancient classical civilizations was also included in the eclectic conglomeration of classical revival styles.

Architectural compendiums duplicating antique designs, styles, and types were soon available to students of neoclassical design theory. Many of these sources were interpretations of antique models; however, antique classical models that were included in these volumes were usually basic replications of plans and models and not subject to radical modifications. One important early nineteenth century influence on European students was the teachings of J.-N.-L. Durand, a professor of architecture at the Paris Ecole Polytechnique who compiled two particularly influential volumes of resource materials and theories, *Précis des lecons d'architecture données á l'Ecole Polytechnique* (1802-1805) and *Recueil et parallèle des èdifices en tout genre, anciens et modernes* (1800). These volumes had a significant impact upon the formulation of architectural theory and design throughout the nineteenth century in Europe, and eventually in America as well. In America itself, sourcebooks such as John Haviland's *Practical Builder's Assistant* (1818-1821) and Asher Benjamin's *The American Builder's Companion* (1827) included Greek architectural orders and advice on proper proportions. In his preface, Haviland assured his readers that the examples he used were sanctioned by the most judicious professors. These early architectural guidebooks were rapidly followed by many others that included generous portions of diagrams and advice on the application of classical sources to American design.

Some eighteenth and nineteenth century sourcebooks referred to classical designs in the Vitruvian style. Vitruvius, who lived in first century BC Rome, had written as a handbook for Roman builders a treatise entitled *De Architectura*, based primarily upon Greek prototypes. The author and his work had been an important source for architectural designs and theories concerning Roman and Greek buildings from the Renaissance up to modern times based on recurring translations and interpretations of his famous study. Indeed, the influence of Vitruvius in America would be felt into the twentieth century, as evidenced by a 1914 translation by Professor Morris Hickey Morgan which was extremely influential in encouraging turn-of-the-century American architectural students to study and learn from this ancient authority.

An enormously compelling reason as to why the classical revival styles became especially popular in the memorial arts is because they were seen as the reflection of a timeless ideal and a divine logic which blended intellectual with aesthetic appeal. The persistence of classicism thereby assured the patron of the commemorative monument that the classical tradition was not a whimsical fad and that monuments in the style would always be tasteful. It was perhaps emotionally pleasing as well to be eternally associated with an ideal that had been championed by artists, critics, and governments. Aesthetic and intellectual factors were not, however, the only ones significant in influencing patrons and designers of monuments to favor the classical revival styles: other considerations, such as the relative flexibility of scale and the variety of types available also enhanced the popularity of this model. The large selection of available types and options offered sufficient variety to satisfy a range of tastes and finances. The most prevalent memorial types inspired by the classical tradition were the temple, sarcophagus, altar, column, and exedra.[30] The triumphal arch was also occasionally revived, usually as a public memorial.[31]

Temples

Of all classical revival forms, it is the temple model which has arguably inspired the most massive and spectacularly beautiful funerary monuments, as best exemplified through its impact upon mausoleum design. Greek and Roman temples were especially well adapted to mausoleum architecture. Specifically defined, a mausoleum is a building with accessible chamber or chambers within which crypts, vaults, or sarcophagi house the remains of the deceased. There are primarily two types of mausoleums: the first and most numerous is private, built by individuals and usually intended for family use. The other is public and intended for a prominent figure such as an American president; these are usually built by organizations or committees using donated funds and designed to accommodate numbers of visitors.

Though the form was not entirely unknown prior to this time, private mausoleums became increasingly popular in America after the opening of non-sectarian and rural cemeteries, the majority of the earliest examples in this phase dating from the 1840s and 1850s. The Civil War interrupted the impetus for building large family mausoleums; however, there was a strong resurgence of building after the troubled years that followed the war, with the final peak of activity occurring in the first two decades of the twentieth century. The final flowering is dominated by the often spectacular tombs of industrious, self-made millionaires, a generation which grew in numbers at the end of the nineteenth century. Public mausoleums, most often sheltering the remains of American presidents, also increased in popularity after the Civil War.

A wide selection of classical revival types and styles provided abundant architectural designs to satisfy both the public or private functions of mausoleums and the individual tastes of clients and architects. The temple-like character of these memorial structures made them both symbolically appropriate and psychologically acceptable for structures that served as shrines for the dead. The fact that the original ancient temple prototypes were primarily used to worship Greek and Roman pagan deities, a situation seemingly antithetical to the Christian religion, did not seem to matter. Critics of classicism were in fact most often proponents of the Gothic revival, and it was largely in comparing classical with medieval forms that concepts of Christian versus pagan traditions entered into the evaluation. If, indeed, the original sources were pre-Christian, designers and patrons could espouse a neo-Platonic interpretation of these early idealized places of worship. However, it is more probable that a fairly substantial number of nineteenth century patrons never consciously philosophized about the original meaning and use of these antique forms. The designs were practical, pleasing, and popular—reasons enough for designers and patrons to choose them. Design options could run the gamut from clean, pure, geometric formality based upon Greek formulas and Roman prototypes to the grand and elegant sumptuousness of Renaissance revival styles that were influenced by ancient mediterranean classical sources. Although the replication of antique classical Greek and Roman sources could prove to be somewhat pedantically restrictive in regards to creative expression, to many patrons the redundancy of the neoclassical styles was anything but detrimental when applied to family mausoleum designs. There was a desired security in the timelessness of the antique plans; individuality or originality was for homes, mansions, or estates, structures and landscapes for the living which could easily enough be changed with the whims of fashion. Their tombs, on the other hand, would be a part of an aesthetic tradition validated by academicians and recurringly revived by western cultures. To be sure, variations on antique prototypes and manipulation of the Greek and Roman architectural elements provided some creative interpretations of these traditional classical sources; however, there is often a high degree of noticeable redundancy in plan and architectural features in nineteenth and early twentieth century neoclassical mausoleum designs derived from Greek and Roman sources.

Among the Greek plans which most inspired mausoleum designers were temples with columns in antis (having a portico with columns between antae walls or pilasters), peripheral (having a row of free-standing columns on all four sides), prostyle (having columns across the front portico), amphiprostyle (having columns across the front and back), and tholos (circular) plans. Choices of Tuscan, Greek or Roman Doric, Ionic, and Corinthian, as well as composite capitals were used atop fluted or smooth column shafts. Some shafts featured entasis, a swell or bulge in the middle duplicating the elastic, organic quality found in Greek prototypes, while others tapered gradually. Designers who wished to be consistent with the antique orders employed triglyphs and metopes in the entablature when Doric columns were used, while the frieze of the Ionic or Corinthian order was continuous. It

was not uncommon, however, for mausoleum designers to modify or personalize the entablature with features differing from the antique norms.

The Edward William Robinson mausoleum (Fig. 9) in Philadelphia's Laurel Hill Cemetery is an early nineteenth century variation on the antique distyle in antis plan. Designed by John Notman c.1838, the Robinson mausoleum employs Doric columns between antae walls ornamented with twin pilasters. Although it does not have a gabled roof, reference is made to the pediment by the slightly pointed shape of the stone atop the front cornice which bears the Robinson family name. A memorial wreath is the only decoration on the lintel of the modified entablature. Located on a hilly incline, the rear of the mausoleum has been integrated into the cemetery landscape. Notman was an exceptionally versatile architect: born in Edinburgh and educated in Scotland before coming to America in 1831, he had a wide-ranging professional interest in funerary designs, landscape planning, and cemetery design. This expertise is well demonstrated in Notman's overall design plan for Laurel Hill, its colonnaded entrance, and a variety of tombs and other structures within its boundaries. In addition to Laurel Hill, he planned Hollywood Cemetery in Richmond, Virginia (1848) and laid out the original plan of Cincinnati's Spring Grove Cemetery in 1845, which was later modified to better suit the peculiarities of the site's landscape. Several of his designs, including the Robinson mausoleum, are featured in an 1844 *Guide to Laurel Hill Cemetery, Near Philadelphia*, written by John Jay Smith, a founder of Laurel Hill. Smith's *Guide*, along with his 1846 *Designs for Monuments and Mural Tablets Adapted to Rural Cemeteries and Churchyards*, offers relevant insights into current attitudes regarding the funerary arts and cemetery design during the premier stages of American endeavors in these areas.

A conventional facsimile of the Greek distyle in antis formula is provided in the John W. Sterling mausoleum (Fig. 10), located in Woodlawn Cemetery, the Bronx, New York.

Fig. 9. Edward William Robinson mausoleum, Laurel Hill Cemetery, Philadelphia. Photo by Peggy McDowell.

Designed by the McKim, Mead and White firm and built in 1910 at a cost of $24,000, the Sterling mausoleum employs the typical features of the Doric order with triglyphs and metopes in the entablature frieze and a pediment decorated with acroteria.

Both the 1850 Miltenberger tomb and the 1842 Peniston-Duplantier mausoleum in St. Louis Cemetery II, New Orleans (Fig. 11), were based on the prostyle design, that is, a building with front portico supported by free-standing columns. These tombs were designed by Jacques Nicolas Bussiere de Pouilly, a French born and educated architect who moved to New Orleans in 1833. Tombs designed by de Pouilly were probably inspired by monuments found in Père Lachaise and by the teachings of J.-N.-L. Durand. The majority of de Pouilly's designs of this type employ a low podium with front steps leading to a shallow portico which features a pedimented roof supported by two columns of a Greek order. The main structure may (as in the Peniston family mausoleum) or may not (as in the Miltenberger family tomb) provide a shallow chamber preceding the vaults. Whenever this chamber was employed, iron or bronze doors closed the entrance. The chambered type was common to Père Lachaise and frequently illustrated in books treating this and other Parisian cemeteries, and de Pouilly is believed to have owned such a book of illustrations devoted to Père Lachaise. An additional typical feature of de Pouilly's designs that was also commonly found in Parisian cemeteries of the period is the use of an iron fence to surround the monument. Fences in wrought and cast iron were popularly used in New Orleans cemeteries and often defined the boundaries of the family plot, but de Pouilly was particularly sensitive to use a design that complemented the tomb. Iron fences surrounding his classical revival designs are simple, with geometrical order and repetition; others, inspired by Gothic or Egyptian revival styles, employ decorative elements consistent with those styles. De Pouilly's original ideas for designs can be studied from material contained in a sketchbook that is in the holdings of The Historic New Orleans Collection. From the numerous drawings therein devoted primarily to tombs and other funerary monuments, one may reasonably conclude that de Pouilly and his clients preferred the Classical revival over Egyptian and Gothic revival designs. However, a review of his work reveals that this versatile architect employed all three revival styles with equal efficiency.[32]

The William G. Helis mausoleum (Fig. 12), located in Metairie Cemetery, New Orleans, is an example of the amphiprostyle plan, with Ionic columns on the front and rear. Built in the mid-twentieth century by the Albert Weiblen firm, the mausoleum was inspired by the Temple of Athena Nike on the Acropolis, and the choice for the design was primarily influenced by Mr. Helis' Greek heritage. Revival style designs continued to be popular in New Orleans well into the twentieth century, and the Weiblen firm by continuing to provide quality builders and designers helped to assure their success. Albert Weiblen immigrated to New Orleans from Germany and began his career as a monument builder in the late nineteenth century. His firm became the primary builder of mausoleums in New Orleans in the first half of the twentieth century, leasing the rights to a major source of granite, the Stone Mountain quarry at Stone Mountain, Georgia.

Two versions of the peripteral temple plan are presented in the Fleischmann mausoleum, Spring Grove Cemetery, Cincinnati, Ohio, and the Jay Gould mausoleum, Woodlawn Cemetery, the Bronx, New York. The Fleischmann tomb (Fig. 13), erected in 1913, employs Doric columns and was inspired by the Parthenon in Athens. Built of light colored granite from the famous quarries at Barre, Vermont, the interior accommodates a chapel with an altar, double sarcophagi, and numerous crypts.

The Gould mausoleum (Fig. 14) is an Ionic peripteral mausoleum designed by H.Q. French of New York and built for financier Jay Gould (1836-1892). John Haviland, in his *Practical Builder's Assistant*, had observed that the "Ionic order is appropriate for churches, colleges, seminaries, libraries, all edifices dedi-

Fig. 10. John W. Sterling mausoleum, Woodlawn Cemetery, the Bronx, New York. Photo by Peggy McDowell.

Fig. 11. Miltenberger tomb (background) and Peniston-Duplantier mausoleum, St. Louis Cemetery II, New Orleans. Photo by Peggy McDowell.

Fig. 12. William G. Helis mausoleum, Metairie Cemetery, New Orleans. Photo by Peggy McDowell.

Fig. 13. Fleischmann mausoleum, Spring Grove Cemetery, Cincinnati. Photo courtesy Spring Grove Cemetery.

cated to literature and the arts, and all places of peace and tranquility."[33] The beauty of the picturesque Woodlawn setting would certainly meet Haviland's requirements for the appropriate use of the Ionic order, and the architect of the Gould mausoleum must have agreed with Haviland's sentiments. *The New York Times*, in its issue of August 18, 1885, notes that Mr. French was a particularly conscientious builder of tombs, and "built those intrusted to him with the utmost care, often causing remark as to his apparent extravagance in using only the choicest materials.... Many of the usual methods of doing this work were rejected and great improvements made.... Mr. French invariably does the whole work, assuming the entire responsibility, and in this manner has obtained a reputation and a success highly deserved."[34] Unfortunately, very little has been written on this exceptional designer of tombs whose structures are located in the cemeteries of numer-

ous American cities. What little we do know suggests that H.Q. French was probably Hamline Q. French, who married Ida Launitz, a member of the family of Robert Launitz, noted sculptor and designer of monuments with whom French had collaborated.

Although the Greeks originally used the central plan design for temples, the central plan mausoleum actually finds its precedence in Roman antiquity, and by extension in early Christian times, where it was used for martyriums and baptisteries. Along with the circular temple surrounded by a colonnade, the Greeks used the octagonal configuration, as demonstrated by the so-called Tower of the Winds in Athens. This structure, which appears in eighteenth century publications such as Stuart and Revett's *Antiquities of Athens*, published in London in 1762, inspired a variety of mausoleum plans, including the Lucca Vaccaro mausoleum (Fig. 15) in New Orleans' Metairie

Fig. 14. Jay Gould mausoleum, Woodlawn Cemetery, the Bronx, New York. Photo by Peggy McDowell.

Fig. 15. Luca Vaccaro mausoleum, Metairie Cemetery, New Orleans. Photo by Peggy McDowell.

Cemetery, built in the 1930s by the Weiblen firm, with the relief carvings executed by a local sculptor, Albert Reiker.

The central plan was frequently used by mausoleum designers in the famous New York architectural firm of McKim, Mead, and White, who were responsible for an impressive number of monumental mausoleums constructed around the turn of the century. Charles Follen McKim, William Rutherford Mead, and Stanford White designed or collaborated with other designers in their firm and with noted sculptors in creating approximately fifty-five commemorative monuments between 1879 and 1919, a number which does not include campus memorials such as gates, fences, sundials, or water fountains.[35] Approximately forty of their commemorative monuments are funerary and include tombstones, memorial tablets, sarcophagi, exedra, and mausoleums, with costs ranging from $50 to $137,040. Although members of the firm occasionally designed a funerary monument with medieval characteristics, such as the gothicized A. C. Honore monument (1905) in Chicago's Graceland Cemetery, the vast majority of their designs were based upon classical sources. Inspirations came from antique temple prototypes, as in the Doric Sterling mausoleum discussed earlier, from classical stele, columns, and sarcophagi, and from Renaissance revival or Beaux-Arts classicism. The majority of the mausoleums actually reflect a type of classicism that is somewhat generic and not specifically borrowed from antique sources but from refined eclectic interpretations of classicism reflecting the Beaux-Arts movement of the late nineteenth and early twentieth century.

Although monuments by McKim, Mead, and White may be found in a number of states, the majority are located in the cemeteries of New York City and its surrounding area. Of those in New York, the firm's mausoleums in the Bronx's Woodlawn Cemetery are particularly impressive and demonstrate the range of neoclassical styles and elegance of taste one associates with America's turn-of-the-century elite classes. Located in Woodlawn are the firm-designed mausoleums of Henry E. Russell (1893), Robert and Ogden Goelet (1897), Henry Augustus Coit Taylor (1900), Louis Sherry (1906), Charles J. Osborn (1908), and the aforementioned John W. Sterling (begun 1910). Depending on scale and types of rare marbles and other materials used, the costs of these structures varied from $3,900 to $137,040,[36] and, of course, it goes without saying that they could never be duplicated for these sums today (if indeed they could be duplicated at all). The least expensive of this group, the Charles J. Osborn tomb (Fig. 16), a circular plan embellished with pilasters, is actually quite elegant and is as visually imposing as the more costly mausoleums. The majority of the classical revival tombs in Woodlawn conceived by this firm are balanced, central plans based on the square, octagon, Greek cross, or circle. Several employ a shallow portico supported by classical columns, and there is also a preference for use of the dome. The designs by McKim, Mead, and White are typical of the types of tombs constructed during the final flowering of grandiose funerary monuments built for the self-made millionaires of the late nineteenth century. At a time when America was suffering from serious economic problems, these affluent elite had ample funds to afford "marble tomb palaces," as they were described by one awed newspaper journalist of the period.

The Henry E. Russell mausoleum (Fig. 17) in Woodlawn was designed by McKim, Mead, and White in 1893-94 at a cost of $25,531.25. The plan is based on an octagonal central chamber from which four pedimented arms (each approximately four feet, ten inches wide) project. One of these arms serves as the portico. The entablature is ornamented with triglyphs and metopes, Doric columns support the portico roof, and acroteria top the pediment and the corners. The courses of stone are neatly aligned and alternate from wide to narrow bands, creating a horizontal rhythm along the surface. This is consistent with the stonework on most of McKim, Mead, and White's Woodlawn designs, which present a refined repetitive granite block alignment. The

Fig. 16. Charles J. Osborn mausoleum, Woodlawn Cemetery, the Bronx, New York. Photo by Peggy McDowell.

Fig. 17. Henry E. Russell mausoleum, Woodlawn Cemetery, the Bronx, New York. Photo by Peggy McDowell.

interior chamber of the Russell mausoleum, similar to most of the designs executed by this firm in Woodlawn, is topped by a mosaic covered dome. Drawings and details of this tomb found in the collection of the New York Historical Society reveal that there was a division of labor within the firm through which a team of specialists coordinated the sculptural and ornamental details with the architectural plan.

Robert and Ogden Goelet were affluent New York real estate developers for whom a residence in the shingled style, an office in the Dutch tradition, and an Italianate office had all been previously designed by members of the McKim, Mead, and White firm. The family mausoleum (Fig. 18) commissioned by the brothers in 1897 and completed in 1899 is a simple and elegant structure in a style that has its origins in antique and Renaissance classicism. The plan is essentially square, elevated on a low podium with a portico supported by fluted Ionic columns. The masonry string courses recall the stonework on the Russell mausoleum. At the uppermost course of the wall, beneath the roof cornice, is a band with triglyph and metope delineation, a feature that combines a Doric characteristic with the Ionic portico. The blueprints are signed by the designer, Samuel P. Hall, who was with the firm from 1895 to 1901.

The Henry Augustus Coit Taylor mausoleum (Fig. 19), designed by McKim, Mead, and White and erected in Woodlawn in 1900, was, at $137,040, one of the most expensive mausoleums undertaken by this firm. Several sheets of drawings in the records of the firm preserved at the New York Historical Society include details of plot, floor plan, furnishings, and decorations. Different signatures appear on these drawings, and the blueprint is signed by Hunter (probably F. Leo Hunter) and dated 1900. The plan is based on an octagonal configuration elevated by a podium, with the upper cornice supported by engaged Corinthian columns. The oculus of a doubled shell dome and a window illuminate the interior.

A fine example of McKim, Mead, and White's classical temple style monuments at Woodlawn is afforded by the Louis Sherry mausoleum (Fig. 20), which features a Greek cross plan with short arms, central dome, and shallow portico supported by two fluted Doric columns. The pedimented portico is adorned by traditional acroteria, with triglyphs limited to the frieze corners. The restrained design is the antithesis of the opulent features evident in Sherry's famous New York hotel and restaurant, which had been created by Stanford White in the late 1890s. White, as one of his last projects before his death in 1909, most probably designed the Sherry mausoleum.

Other mausoleum designers of the period reflected tastes similar to those of McKim, Mead, and White and, like them, created models of grandiose Renaissance and Beaux-Arts temples for the dead in the early twentieth century. The John William Mackay mausoleum (Fig. 21), formally dedicated in 1898, is one of the most impressive tombs in Green-Wood Cemetery, Brooklyn, New York. Its grandeur so astounded a contemporary newspaper columnist from New Orleans that he wrote in the January 23, 1898 issue of the *Times Picayune*: "This now forms one of a group by the side of which the massive remains of Greek and Roman memorial sculpture pale almost into insignificance, at least as far as gorgeousness of effect is concerned." The author goes on to describe the features of the tomb, stating that the main roofstone, with its weight of forty tons and its dimensions of twenty feet, six inches square, and fourteen inches thick, constitutes the largest single piece of stone ever quarried in the United States. The name of the architect who conceived this structure is not known; however, he used design features quite similar to those found in contemporaneous mausoleums designed by McKim, Mead, and White. Like the majority of that firm's mausoleum designs in Woodlawn, the Mackay plan is symmetrical and centrally oriented. It has a dome over the square central chamber with arms that project from the four sides, one of which serves as the entrance. Four bronze statues, cast in Munich, are placed atop these arms and represent, according to

Fig. 18. Robert and Ogden Goelet mausoleum, Woodlawn Cemetery, the Bronx, New York. Photo by Peggy McDowell.

Fig. 19. Henry Augustus Coit Taylor mausoleum, Woodlawn Cemetery, the Bronx, New York. Photo by Peggy McDowell.

Fig. 20. Louis Sherry mausoleum, Woodlawn Cemetery, the Bronx, New York. Photo by Peggy McDowell.

Fig. 21. John William Mackay mausoleum, Green-Wood Cemetery, Brooklyn, New York. Photo by Peggy McDowell.

the *Times Picayune* article, the allegorical figures of Sorrow, Faith, Death, and Life.[37] Harry A. Bliss features the Mackay tomb, which he identifies as a Renaissance design, in a 1912 publication entitled *Memorial Art, Ancient and Modern*, indicating that the mausoleum was designed to be heated and lighted by electricity. The interior, with its twenty-two separate crypts, is enhanced by the use of sumptuous marble, mosaics, and an elaborate altar. John William Mackay (1831-1902) was a fortunate speculator, one of several miners who discovered the Nevada Comstock Lode in 1859, making him a millionaire almost overnight. The Mackay name is also historically important in the founding of the Postal Telegraph and Cable Corporation, an organization which broke the monopoly of Jay Gould's Western Union Telegraph Company.

Tycoons and robber barons were not the only influential Americans to have their memories perpetuated through use of the antique temple model. There was a propensity as well to choose classical revival designs in the creation of commemorative and funerary monuments to former American presidents. Many of their funerary monuments are heavily visited to this day by Americans wishing to pay their respects, and these were in fact designed to accommodate such visitors. Others are more modest and not public-oriented. Though a variety of types appear throughout this study, the monuments that seem best suited to be included in this section are those that display neoclassical temple-like properties. Some of these are funerary, while others are purely commemorative, i.e., a memorial, usually with a statue replacing the emphasis on the body. The site of President Ulysses S. Grant's tomb (Fig. 22), perhaps the most famous neoclassical mausoleum in nineteenth century America, is particularly interesting in that it is both memorial shrine and mausoleum.

Grant, former commanding general of the Union forces during the Civil War and eighteenth President of the United States, died on July 23, 1885, and the Grant Monument Association was formed in February of the following year to supervise the construction of a tomb suitable to house the body of the man idealistically credited with saving and stabilizing the Union. Former president Chester A. Arthur acted as first chairman of the association. Funds were raised through popular subscription, and approximately 90,000 people contributed the $600,000 used to build the General Grant National Memorial. According to *The New York Times*, at least $520,000 of this amount came from New York residents. The rest was contributed from outside the state or constituted interest accumulated on the principal sum invested in New York trust companies.[38]

The Grant Monument Association originally wanted to select the best design from an international competition. As an inducement, prize money was promised for the winning designs as selected by a committee of judges. This contest was extended over a period of years and ultimately resulted in a total of sixty-five entries. At the Association's annual meeting in February, 1890, the five winners were announced, with the top prize of $1,500 awarded to the Washington, D.C. architectural firm of Cluss and Schulze. The motto of their winning design was "Sword and Laurel," and it presented an equestrian statue of Grant in front of a tall shaft. Despite the fanfare, however, the committee of "experts" who judged the entries and made recommendations to the Grant Monument Association had not been overly impressed by the results of the competition. They proposed that prizes be awarded as promised but without commitment to build any of the submitted designs, and the Association honored this recommendation. A second competition was subsequently held, this time by invitation, with five established architects or architectural firms selected and compensated for their designs. The chosen firms and/or individual architects were: Carrere and Hastings; Charles W. Clinton; N. LeBrun and Sons; John H. Duncan, and John Ord.[39]

The Association had meanwhile decided that a memorial hall along with burial facilities for General and Mrs. Grant was the preferred concept, and thus the final group of submitted designs shared many similar features. Four of

Fig. 22. Ulysses S. Grant National Memorial and Mausoleum, New York City. Photo by Peggy McDowell.

them employed a central crypt topped by a dome, three of these being directly inspired by Napoleon's tomb at the Invalides in Paris. The design submitted by John H. Duncan was the overwhelming choice of the Executive Committee of the Association, the members of which were particularly impressed by the fact that Duncan had examined the site of the tomb and had planned his design to best suit the environment. The New York City location had previously been selected along the Hudson River in Riverside Park, where a temporary vault was built to preserve the remains of the former president until a proper tomb could be constructed (an attempt by the federal government to move Grant's body to Arlington National Cemetery had been thwarted). The motivations to keep Grant's remains in New York, one of three places chosen as a possible burial site by the former president himself before he died, recall the traditions of the medieval pilgrimage, with Grant's body replacing the religious relic. The Manhattan site made the burial place more accessible to New York residents, and the inclusion of a memorial chamber within the tomb transformed the monument into a museum and a shrine that could accommodate numerous visitors. The Association concluded that Duncan's design best suited both the function and the site, and was ideally impressive from all vantage points: its members also felt it important that the proposed monument looked like a mausoleum rather than an "inhabited" building, and that the architect's plan "recalls less strongly any building already extant."[40] Practical considerations which also made Duncan's design acceptable included the fact that it could be built for the available money and in phases over a period of years, as presented by the architect's master plan.

The foundation was laid on April 27, 1891, and the mausoleum dedicated six years to the day later, on April 27, 1897 (the timing was in fact quite deliberate: Grant's birthday was April 27, a date often celebrated by the Monument Association). The tomb is constructed of pale gray granite quarried in North Jay, Maine, and the utmost care was taken to insure that the blocks of granite selected were without flaws. The building itself recalls the monumental grandeur of the Mausoleum of Halicarnnassus and of Roman imperial tombs (it has been likened, for instance, to Hadrian's tomb). The design, however, was not copied from any specific ancient monument, representing, rather, a somewhat heavy-handed eclectic combination of classical forms. With its geometric severity and rigorous articulation of parts, the structure lacks any Greek-inspired organic subtleties or elasticity: its weighty bulk, however, seems most admirably suitable for a funerary monument. The square building, elevated on a podium, has an unpedimented front portico supported by columns of the Doric order. Doric columns within recessed niches are placed on the other sides, helping to create a harmonious balance with the facade and ornament otherwise austere walls. An entablature separates the lower level from an upper level, and on the front center top, the focal emphasis of a high truncated pediment is a timely inscription—"Let Us Have Peace"—flanked by sculptures representing War and Peace created by the sculptor J. Massey Rhind. This inscription, taken from a letter by Grant in which he accepted the Republican nomination for President, and which also subsequently became the campaign slogan for the party, had actually been previously submitted as a motto by one of the finalists in the first design competition. Atop the massive square portion of the tomb stands a circular colonnade that elevates stepped graduated ring courses of stone, resulting in a conical shape over the center of the mausoleum. The circular configuration has its basis in an ancient Greek design, the tholos, and is found as well in Roman architecture; it is, however, also strongly associated with the Renaissance. On the interior of the structure is a central dome which forms a canopy over the circular crypt, visible through an opening in the main floor and containing the sarcophagi of President and Mrs. Grant. The sarcophagi themselves are constructed of large, heavy blocks of specially selected red porphyry stone quarried in Montello, Wisconsin and placed on granite bases from Quincy, Massachusetts.

The tomb also serves as a military memorial, and there is a great emphasis placed upon Ulysses S. Grant the general. His tenure as President between 1869 and 1877 is, in fact, not as obviously represented among the tomb's paraphernalia as objects or images pertaining to his role as commander of the Union army. The interior of the tomb originally included military trophy rooms, with maps of important Civil War battles accompanied by appropriate paintings, reliefs, and battle flags. While these original displays are no longer intact, two small corner rooms are currently used for exhibits. Busts of five collaborating Union generals—Sheridan, Sherman, McPherson, Ord, and Thomas—are placed in niches around the wall of the crypt, while allegorical relief figures on the pendentives represent Grant's early years, military career, presidency, and death.

The mausoleum of William McKinley (Fig. 23) was also built from funds donated by the American public. McKinley, who began his tenure as twenty-fifth President of the United States in 1897, was assassinated in 1901 while serving a second term, and his body was returned for burial to Canton, Ohio, the city that had been his home for many years. Funds amounting to more than $570,000 were collected by the McKinley National Memorial Association, and a design competition was won by Harold Van Buren Magonigle of New York, a former employee of McKim, Mead, and White. Work on the tomb began in June, 1905, and its dedication took place in September of 1907. The McKinley mausoleum, adjacent to Canton's Westlawn Cemetery, commands an imposing position above the surrounding landscape. The circular plan is elevated on Monument Hill, with an impressive flight of stairs which span the width of the building extending down the slope of the hill in front (the landscape plan originally included a cascading basin, called the Long Water, situated at the foot of the hill). The total effect of the ground plan, which is readable only from an aerial layout, is a design based on the motif of a cross-hilted sword, with the tomb at the center, or hilt, of the cross. The tomb itself is an austere, cylindrical building topped by a dome with an opening at its apex in the tradition of the Roman Pantheon. In the center of the main room, which is shaped like a Greek cross, lie the sarcophagi of William and Ida McKinley. The overall design is reminiscent of Roman architectural traditions and recalls the sixth century tomb of Theodoric in Ravenna.

Besides serving as mausoleums, buildings resembling classical temples were also used for other commemorative purposes, again frequently being designed and built with monies raised through public subscription. In Washington D.C., the Lincoln Memorial (Fig. 24), built in the early 1920s from a design by Henry Bacon, and the Jefferson Memorial (Fig. 25), designed by John Russell Pope and built in 1943, were also inspired by neoclassical idealism. These immediately recognizable elements of the Washington landscape complement the classical features of the nearby Capitol and White House, and it is difficult to envision them in any style other than classical revival even though they were both constructed well into the twentieth century. Although not specifically funerary, such memorials were often emotionally equated with surrogate tombs, monumental cenotaphs made accessible and visible to the general public in order to educate and induce continuing respect. And because the classical styles evoke the ideals of logic and order, it may be theoretically inferred that they are intended to reflect both the temperament of the person commemorated and the government which erected the monument. Perhaps this as much as anything accounts for the close association of classical revival styles, both funerary and otherwise, with American authority figures and political institutions.

Antique Greek and Roman temples also frequently served as prototypes for monuments to the memory of those who served and died in battle. One such commemorative monument is located on Riverside Drive in New York City, not far from Grant's tomb (Fig. 26). With its Corinthian columns and tall, vertically compact quality, this circular structure, known as the Soldiers and Sailors Monument, resembles

Fig. 23. William McKinley mausoleum, Canton, Ohio. Photo courtesy Ohio Historical Society.

Fig. 24. Lincoln Memorial, Washington, D.C. Photo courtesy Library of Congress.

Fig. 25. Jefferson Memorial, Washington, D.C. Photo courtesy Library of Congress.

Fig. 26. Soldiers and Sailors Monument, New York City. Photo by Peggy McDowell.

both the antique tholos temple and the Monument of Lysicrates in Athens. Designed by Charles W. and Arthur A. Stoughton, the monument was dedicated on Memorial Day, 1902. A sad reminder of the manner in which values have changed since that time is afforded by the many and repeated instances of vandalism in the form of garish, spray-painted graffiti which in recent years have defaced the surface of the monument.

Monuments situated in Civil War battlefields may also occasionally emulate classical temples. It is often an unexpected shock to visitors touring these landscapes, former pastures and fields of battle, to suddenly come upon one of these structures that so vividly conjure up images of a time and place far removed from the current context. A particularly striking instance of this phenomenon is apparent when one visits the rural picturesque setting at Vicksburg National Military Park in Vicksburg, Mississippi, and finds the Illinois Monument (Fig. 27), which was inspired by the Roman Pantheon. Designed by William L. A. Jenney and dedicated in 1906, the white marble building, with eagles and other emblems of America ornamenting the exterior, features a portico, circular cella, and unglazed oculus. The floor is inlaid with mosaic patterns, and bronze tablets around the interior wall list the names of the Illinois men who fought at Vicksburg.

Classical Canopies and Related Structures

The circular plan of the standard temple design was frequently modified to suit the particular needs of commemorative architecture. One such variation produced a domed canopy or cupola supported by columns. Although prototypes can be found in ancient Roman memorials, such as the cupola on the so-called Tomb of the Julii at Saint-Rémy in Provence, the concept was more recently popular in eighteenth century garden pavilions. The design provided shelter and at the same time was open to allow for an interaction between space under the cupola and the exterior, thus rendering it an ideal and functional configuration in a garden or landscape setting. The advantages of the garden kiosk were soon recognized by monument designers, who most often utilized the cupola in funerary designs to shelter a grave and its marker or monument without the confinement or restriction of walls interfering with the visibility of the site. Such a configuration, it was understood, invites interaction between viewer and monument. Andrew Jackson (1767-1845), seventh President of the United States, and his wife, Rachel, rest beneath a domed circular monument of this type (Fig. 28) in the gardens of The Hermitage, Jackson's home near Nashville, Tennessee. The modest domed cupola is supported by Doric columns that encircle a small obelisk atop a pedestal. On either side of the pedestal are two flat slabs that mark the graves of the president and his wife. The inscription to Rachel, who died in 1828, describes Andrew's love and admiration for his wife. The history of their love affair and marriage before a divorce had been granted from Rachel's first husband had been frequently used by Jackson's political opponents to denounce the couple and imply a lack of morality or good character. Even though Andrew and Rachel had originally married in good faith, believing that the divorce had been approved by the Virginia legislature, Rachel's name was as a consequence frequently associated with infidelity, abandonment, and adultery. After the divorce petition filed by Rachel's first husband was eventually granted, a second marriage ceremony rectified the situation, and the Jacksons lived together for almost forty years before her death. Rachel's character was defended even after her death, however, as her commemorative inscription includes the phrase: "A being so gentle and so virtuous, slanders might wound, but could not dishonor; even death, when he bore her from the arms of her husband, could but transport her to the bosom of God." The elegant simplicity of the Jackson monument in its landscape setting is totally in harmony with the classicism of The Hermitage as a whole.

Fig. 27. Illinois Monument, Vicksburg National Military Park, Vicksburg, Mississippi. Photo courtesy U.S. Army Corps of Engineers.

Fig. 28. Andrew Jackson Monument, The Hermitage, near Nashville, Tennessee. Photo by Grannis, Nashville.

A variation of this type, the peribolus, employs the circular colonnade without a dome or roof of any kind. The monument to former President Warren G. Harding (1865-1923) and his wife, Florence, in Marion, Ohio (Fig. 29), employs the domeless circular colonnade on a grand scale. The design looks like a classical Stonehenge, if one can imagine such a cromlech. One hundred and three feet wide, the colonnade encircles the burial plot of the former president and his first lady. A freestanding exterior colonnade consisting of Doric columns twenty-eight feet high and five feet in diameter at the base encloses a circular wall with an interior Ionic peristyle. The Ionic columns are positioned around the grassy burial plot, which is left open to the elements.[41] A national competition was held by the Harding Memorial Association in 1925, with the winning design submitted by Henry F. Hornbostel and Eric Fisher Wood of Pittsburgh. According to the *Harding Memorial Dedication Program*, dated June 17, 1931, a total of $977,821.76 was raised by popular subscription to build the monument.

Along with circular plans, square and rectangular structures with entablatures supported by classical columns, with or without roofs, were also used to enclose or define burial areas. The monument to former President James Knox Polk (1795-1849) and his wife, Sara Childress Polk (Fig. 30), is covered by such a rectangular canopy. Four simple classical columns support an unadorned roof over an inscribed square pedestal. James K. Polk had moved to Tennessee from his native North Carolina, and after serving as governor of Tennessee was elected to become the eleventh President of the United States. Following their deaths, the tomb of Polk and his wife was originally erected on the family estate, but was later moved to the grounds of the Tennessee State Capitol in Nashville when the Polk home was demolished. William Strickland designed the monument, emulating a pattern he had previously used in a monument for Alfred Theodore Miller in Philadelphia's Laurel Hill Cemetery. The Miller structure (Fig. 31) shelters a sculpted image of a reclining child, pre-sumably a portrait of the seven-month-old Alfred, rendered, according to the 1844 *Guide to Laurel Hill*, by "the celebrated sculptor Pettrich." The monument itself was erected sometime around 1840 by John Struthers, who often executed Strickland's designs.

The Potter Palmer monument (Fig. 32) in Chicago's Graceland Cemetery is a particularly stately version of the rectangular canopy form. Begun and built between 1904 and 1906 by contractor C.B. Blake, from the design by McKim, Mead, and White, this large structure supported by Ionic columns shelters two matching sarcophagi about nine feet in height. The scroll lids of these sarcophagi recall the Roman Scipio's sarcophagus (see next section), with swags and inverted torches ornamenting the ends and sides. The design was probably commissioned by Bertha Palmer for herself and her husband, who died in 1902. The choice of McKim, Mead, and White, as in the previously mentioned case of the Louis Sherry mausoleum in New York City, would seem the act of a satisfied patron, as the firm had previously designed an addition to the Palmer residence in 1892 to serve as an art gallery.

Military monuments also used the canopy form to create a memorial shrine. The Pennsylvania State Memorial (Fig. 33), dedicated in 1910 on the Gettysburg battlefield, combines the triumphal arch motif with the centralized domed canopy. The square memorial presents a monumental triumphal arch on each of its four faces, while towering above the structure is an imposing dome that in turn supports a monumental allegorical figure representing a Nike or Goddess of Peace. The association of the image of Victory, Nike, to triumph seems fitting, for it is supported by triumphal arches. The structure is elevated on a square podium, and around the base of the nine foot parapet are placed bronze tablets with the names of those Pennsylvanians who served in the battle. According to the guidebook, the base of the memorial is eighty feet square and the height to the top of the statue measures 110 feet.[42]

Fig. 29. Warren G. Harding Monument, Marion, Ohio. Photo courtesy Ohio Historical Society.

Fig. 30. James Knox Polk Monument, Nashville, Tennessee. Photo by Grannis, Nashville.

Fig. 31. Alfred Theodore Miller monument, Laurel Hill Cemetery, Philadelphia. Photo by Harold Allen.

Fig. 32. Potter Palmer monument, Graceland Cemetery, Chicago. Photo by Robert Wright.

Fig. 33. Pennsylvania Monument, Gettysburg National Military Park, Gettysburg, Pennsylvania. Photo by Peggy McDowell.

Classical Sarcophagi, Altars, and Related Monuments

The sarcophagus is a traditional form of burial furniture. The word "sarcophagus" translated from the Greek literally means "flesh-eater," after a particular type of limestone coffin known for its caustic properties, but later came to be applied to any cut stone burial receptacle in which a body was contained. Inspired by both Greek and Etruscan prototypes, the Romans developed ornate variations of the sarcophagus form. Although reclining figures atop the lid were also popular, the Romans, like the Greeks, favored architectural lids with gabled roofs ornamented by acroteria. To complete the architectural effect, engaged columns or pilasters were occasionally duplicated along the sides or at the corners. The sarcophagus was employed by the early Christians and was later adapted to period styles from the Middle Ages through the Renaissance. In the eighteenth century, Piranesi, fascinated as he was by Roman antiquity, illustrated numerous sarcophagi. Often augmented by his imaginative vision, Piranesi's depictions of sarcophagi can be seen in works such as Volumes I and II of his *Le Antichità Romane* and the *Grotteschi* series. Encouraged by the popularity of nineteenth century neo-classicism, designers revived the antique sarcophagus as a major form of funerary art. The design was exceptionally practical and could either be used within a tomb or constructed as an independent monument. It could be ornamented or left simple, depending on the taste and wealth of the client, and could also be designed with a single vault or expanded to include multiple vaults. J.-N.-L. Durand illustrated numerous examples of Roman sarcophagi in his *Recueil et parallèle des èdifices* (1800), while John Haviland's *Practical Builder's Assistant* (1830) offered American builders and students of architecture a design for a tomb based upon the classical sarcophagus with pediment and acroteria.

The monument to Commodore Isaac Hull erected in Philadelphia's Laurel Hill Cemetery (Fig. 34) is copied from the Roman Scipio (L.

Cornelius Scipio Barbatus) sarcophagus housed in the Vatican Museum. The Hull version, its design attributed to William Strickland and carved by John Struthers, is ornamented by an alert but badly weathered eagle. The Scipio sarcophagus, it should be noted, was extensively copied in nineteenth and twentieth century designs: another version, for example, can be found near the Hull monument in Laurel Hill, in this instance personalized for the use of Mary Barton Cooke.

The Foucher Family tomb in St. Louis Cemetery II in New Orleans (Fig. 35) is a somewhat generic version of a sarcophagus and was probably inspired by similar types found in Paris' Père Lachaise Cemetery. It was designed by the French-born J.N.B de Pouilly, who, as noted earlier, was familiar with the Parisian monuments as well as the sarcophagi illustrated in Durand's *Recueil et parallèle des èdifices*. Inverted torches, such as those seen here on the Foucher sarcophagus, were frequently employed as symbolic decorations on early nineteenth century monuments in Parisian cemeteries, and de Pouilly often incorporated this motif, which can be traced to antique Roman sarcophagi, into the decorative scheme of his tomb designs.

In the later years of the nineteenth century, more ornately carved and footed sarcophagi were introduced into the repertory of American commemorative types. An example of such an ornate configuration is afforded in the 1894 Benjamin Head Warder monument (Fig. 36), located in Rock Creek Cemetery, Washington, D.C., and attributed to Stanford White of the McKim, Mead, and White firm.

A square, block-like monument topping a grave was another prevalent configuration in nineteenth century funerary design and iconography. Commemorative prints, advertisements for cemetery marble works, and death notices were frequently illustrated with a square monument topped by an urn. Cubic monuments placed atop graves were commonly marked with names, dates, and other inscriptions and occasionally decorated along the sides with relief sculpture or architectural motifs. Such square altars and commemorative

Fig. 34. Isaac Hull monument, Laurel Hill Cemetery, Philadelphia. Photo by Clarkson Schoettle, courtesy Friends of Laurel Hill Cemetery.

Fig. 35. Foucher Family tomb, St. Louis Cemetery II, New Orleans. Photo by Peggy McDowell.

Fig. 36. Benjamin Head Warder monument, Rock Creek Cemetery, Washington, D.C. Photo by Peggy McDowell.

markers have their origins in Greek and Roman art. In ancient Rome, for instance, altars were found in funerary complexes as a site for commemorative rituals for the dead. Durand's *Recueil et parallèle des èdifices* illustrates a variety of these Roman altar types, along with a number of examples of sarcophagi (see Fig. 37), and a comparison between Durand's illustrations and nineteenth century commemorative monuments such as the George Whitefield cenotaph in the First Presbyterian Church of Newburyport, Massachusetts (Fig. 38),[43] reveals obvious parallels between antique and revival classical forms. The Whitefield cenotaph was designed in 1828-29 by William Strickland and was executed by John Struthers.[44]

Strickland's teacher, Benjamin Latrobe, had also designed funerary monuments using a heavy square block as the basic form, as may be seen in his design for the monument com-

memorating Eliza Lewis, first wife of Louisiana Governor William C.C. Claiborne, in St. Louis Cemetery I, New Orleans (Fig. 39). The monument is square, with a low relief inlay on one side which depicts Eliza Claiborne and her three-year-old daughter on their death bed (both had died on the same day). At the head of the bed is a Roman fasces, an emblem of authority: an angel hovers over the bodies and holds a crown of immortality while motioning towards heaven. At one time, anthemion decorated acroteria were placed at the corners, which served to reduce the austere effect of the low pyramidal top. A watercolor by Latrobe now in the Library of Congress and labeled "Congressional Cemetery, Washington, D.C." (Fig. 40), illustrates the design of a monument in the foreground which bears great similarity to that of the Claiborne tomb. The three-step foundation, inlays and acroteria of the Claiborne monument are also featured in

Fig. 37. Examples of Roman altars and sarcophagi, from *Recueil et parallèle des édifices en tout genre, anciens et modernes*, by J.N.L Durand.

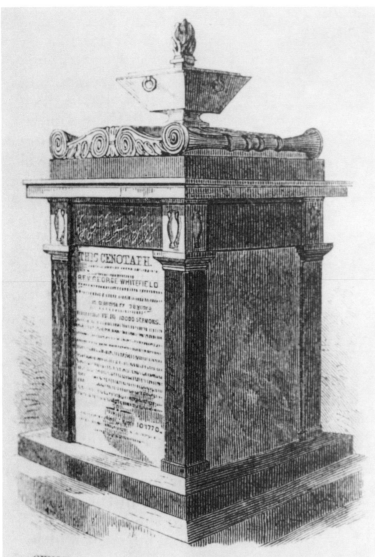

CENOTAPH IN MEMORY OF GEORGE WHITEFIELD.
VOL. LI.—No. 302.—**12**

Fig. 38. Illustration of the Whitefield cenotaph, First Presbyterian Church, Newburyport, Massachusetts. From *Harper's New Monthly Magazine* (1875).

the watercolor design, along with the Roman fasces motif. It is, however, the square markers (or cenotaphs) visible in the background of this watercolor study that, with their austere lines and bulky weight, are actually more typical of the design conceived by Latrobe for the Congressional Cemetery (see Fig. 41). Writing in 1819, he emphasized: "The monument I always recommend to be made of as few blocks as possible, and those of as great weight as the form permits. Of this kind is the monument designed by me for members of Congress who die in Washington and now adopted as mark-

ing their public character."[45] Latrobe had, in effect, refined his Congressional monuments to their essential form, and in so doing eliminated any overt classical details. The prototype for his square monuments probably came from English sources, however: a painting in London's National Gallery by John Constable depicts a cenotaph to the memory of the famous painter Sir Joshua Reynolds (d. 1792) which is quite similar to the Latrobe designs.

The square monument proved to be desirably versatile because it could be easily modified with surface relief decoration and it could serve as a pedestal or podium. The grave of former President Grover Cleveland (1837-1908) in Princeton, New Jersey, is marked by a traditional square monument with pilasters on the corners and an urn finial. And Daniel Boone's grave in the Frankfort Cemetery, Frankfort, Kentucky, was marked in 1859 with a square monument (Fig. 42) which resembles more a classical pedestal than an antique altar. The Boone monument was featured in an 1877 article in *The American Architect and Building News*, wherein the author reflected prevailing American sentiment when he described Boone as "the bravest and most attractive character in all American history," a "venerable Western god."[46] The Kentucky legislature in 1845 adopted measures to have the remains of Daniel Boone, who had died in 1820 at his home in Missouri, and his wife, Rebecca removed from their burial places in Missouri and reinterred in Frankfort, and the Boone Monument Association was established by the legislature in 1848 for the purpose of erecting a monument at the site of his burial so that citizens of Kentucky could show their respect and gratitude to the Boone family as the first Kentucky pioneers.[47] The monument was designed by Robert E. Launitz of New York at a cost of $2,000 and was executed by Stonemason John Haly of Frankfort utilizing

Fig. 39. Claiborne monument, St. Louis Cemetery I, New Orleans. Photo by Peggy McDowell.

locally quarried stone. Italian marble reliefs illustrating significant events in Boone's life were inserted on the four sides, carved under Launitz's direction by a sculptor identified only as Mr. Korwan.

Like the square monument, the table or bench monument easily lent itself to classical ornamentation. One variation popular from the early nineteenth to the early twentieth century employed four or six free-standing marble balusters supporting a rectangular slab. Monuments of this type were frequently used in the eastern portions of the country, though examples found as well in the midwest and the south indicate that the type was probably a nineteenth century stock pattern duplicated and sold throughout the United States (see Fig. 43). This conclusion is further sustained by the fact that the balustrated table monument is frequently featured in nineteenth century advertisements for marble works in city directories and in other publications about cemeteries (e.g., Fig. 44). Benjamin Latrobe had serious doubts concerning the endurance

of this monument type. In his notes of March, 1819, he wrote: "But as if ingenuity had been employed to invent a monument still more caduceous (sic) there has been of late a new fashion introduced."[48] Latrobe continues by providing a clear description of the balustrated table monument and includes a drawing to further clarify its form. It is, of course, true that an obvious problem of the design lies in the unprotected exposure of the elevated slab, usually carved with an inscription, to the elements. Unless the slab were of exceptionally sturdy stone and featured deeply incised lettering or design, it would prove especially vulnerable to deterioration.

Despite Latrobe's concern, however, the table monument continued to be popular. In 1909, by order of Congress, the remains of the architect who envisioned the basic plan of Washington, D.C., Pierre Charles L'Enfant (1754-1825), were moved to a prominent location in front of the Custis-Lee mansion (Arlington House) in Arlington National Cemetery, where his grave, unveiled May 22,

Fig. 40. Benjamin Latrobe watercolor, labeled "Congressional Cemetery, Washington, D.C." Photo courtesy Library of Congress.

Fig. 41. Monuments in the Congressional Cemetery, Washington, D.C. Photo by Peggy McDowell.

Fig. 42. Daniel Boone monument, Frankfort Cemetery, Frankfort, Kentucky. Photo courtesy Frankfort Department of Public Information.

Fig. 43. Nineteenth century table or bench monuments, Holly Springs Cemetery, Holly Springs, Mississippi. Photo by Peggy McDowell.

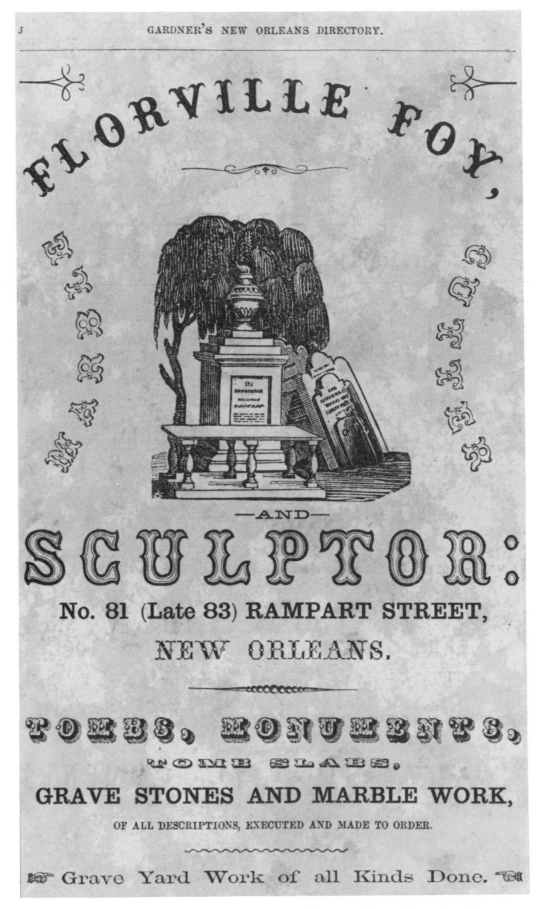

Fig. 44. Monument advertisement, New Orleans, featuring table and other monument styles. Photo courtesy Historic New Orleans Collection.

1911, is marked with a balustrated table monument (Fig. 45). Congress had made a special appropriation of $1,000 to remove the remains of L'Enfant from Green Hill, Prince George County, Maryland, reinter him in Washington, and erect an appropriate monument to his memory. Decisions regarding specific site and design of the monument were placed in the hands of the Commissioners of the District of Columbia, directed by the Secretary of War and aided by the U.S. Army officer in charge of National Cemeteries. M.L. Flavey was the contractor in charge of the work: the name of the designer, however, is not clarified in the records available from Arlington. The Commissioners were present when the remains were disinterred to be transferred to Washington Pierre on April 22, 1909. They were temporarily placed in a vault at Mt. Olivet Cemetery in the District, where they remained until April 28 when they were conveyed with

military escort to the Capitol to lie in state in the morning, with reburial taking place that afternoon. The 1911 dedication ceremonies for the newly erected monument were a grand affair, with President William Howard Taft in attendance to present the dedication address. The monument is erected on a base measuring ten feet, ten inches by six feet, eleven and one-half inches by eleven inches. Atop this stands the monument itself, approximately eight feet by four feet, with four supporting posts approximately one foot, eight inches tall and six inches in diameter at the thickest point. In relief on the lower slab is a broadsword with a garland entwined at the hilt. The top slab is approximately seven feet, six inches long by three feet, seven inches wide and six inches thick. The top, badly weathered, is decorated around the edge with a scalloped pattern and engraved with a circular plan of the City of Washington and an inscription providing basic

Fig. 45. Pierre Charles L'Enfant monument, Arlington National Cemetery, Washington, D.C. Photo courtesy Arlington National Cemetery.

details concerning L'Enfant's life and death. Although the inscription gives the wrong military rank for L'Enfant, it was decided to leave it as carved for fear of damaging the monument.[49]

Another common version of the table monument recalls the more traditional enclosed box with classical pilasters in relief along the sides or on the corners. This form also seems to have inspired nineteenth century stock editions in various dimensions and featuring a number of classicized details. Much like the sarcophagus, which it resembles, this type continued to be popular in the early twentieth century. The Tomb of the Unknown Soldiers erected after World War I in Arlington National Cemetery (Fig. 46) is an excellent example of this variation. The architect of the monument, located at the top of a flight of stairs in front of the Memorial Amphitheater, was Lorimer Rich, its sculptor Thomas Hudson Jones, and the contractors Hagerman and Harris of New York City (the names of the sculptor and architect are inscribed on the lower base). The original Unknown Soldier was selected in 1921 from among four unidentified servicemen who had died in combat in France. A single candidate for the honor was chosen from each of the four American military cemeteries in France— Meuse-Argonne, St. Mihiel, Somme, and Aisne-Marne—and placed in an identical casket: from these anonymous four, an army representative then chose one to represent all the unknown American servicemen who had died in World War I. The remains were transported with military ceremony to Washington, D.C., where, on November 9, 1921, they were placed in the rotunda of the United States Capitol. Thousands of citizens paid their respects before the casket was carried to Arlington for official burial ceremonies on Armistice Day, November 11. There, the remains were placed in a temporary tomb that served until the permanent version replaced it. The present monument, started in August, 1931, was carved from a solid, fifty-ton block of stone (Yule marble) which had been quarried in Colorado and transported to Vermont for rough carving.

Final work was completed on site the following year. The base measures approximately eight feet in width and fourteen feet, eleven inches in length. The rectangular, box-like severity of the tomb is relieved by pilastera in relief at the corners and along the sides, where, within separate panels created by the pilasters, are placed a series of wreaths. Three figures representing Victory, Valor, and Peace are carved on the end of the tomb facing Washington. On the opposite end, facing the Amphitheater, one finds the well-known inscription:

HERE RESTS IN
HONORED GLORY
AN AMERICAN
SOLDIER
KNOWN BUT TO GOD

The original cost of the tomb was $48,000. It was completed and opened to the public on April 9, 1932, and since that time burials of other unknown American military dead from later campaigns have added to the symbolic importance of the original monument.[50]

Columns

Architects devoted to Roman classicism had adequate inspiration for the use of the column as a monument. Examples such as the columns of Hadrian and Trajan and various other commemorative or trophy columns employed by the ancient Romans were frequently illustrated in architectural studies. The antique column was associated with commemoration and victory, ideas that certainly appealed to American designers. In the conception of the column as a monument, sculpture and architectural design merge: architects viewed the column as a structural three-dimensional entity, and sculptors regularly designed and used columns in their sculptural schemes. The column frequently became a megalithic pedestal that elevated a bronze or stone figure to lofty heights. The base, dado, or podium offered other potentials: it could be used as a chamber, for instance, or it could be extended in various directions to multiply the possibili-

Fig. 46. Tomb of the Unknown Soldiers, Arlington National Cemetery, Washington, D.C. Photo by Peggy McDowell.

ties for supporting sculptural figures. A late nineteenth century article in *The American Architect and Building News* describes the merits of the column by contrasting it with the obelisk: "Columns having a wider significance and a larger relationship with human sentiment have taken their places in modern monumental art with no little appropriateness. They are of a higher order of aspiration than the obelisk, and receive decoration with striking grace.... Next to the human and animal forms it suggests the greatest variety of line and movement. It is all curve in every direction, and when decorated according to its character it becomes the object of richest beauty."[51] Numerous columns sprang up across America in the nineteenth and early twentieth centuries, though the majority were erected between 1870 and 1900. A summary analysis of their primary use as monuments in the nineteenth century includes columns that were dedicated to historical figures, columns marking the sites of Revolutionary or Civil War battles, urban columns commemorating those who served and died in these wars, and funerary columns used within cemeteries.

The classical column—as well as the comparable Egyptian obelisk—offered designers an opportunity to achieve great height while employing fairly simple construction principles. Nineteenth century designers often responded to the public's expressed interest in impressive height. As a result, columns and obelisks grew to awesome vertical scale and, all too frequently, boring redundancy. Some of these monuments had interior stairs and observation platforms so that another aspect of height could be exploited: sensationalism merged with memorialization as the public enjoyed the venture of the ascent, view from the top, and descent in these columns which doubled as observation towers. This additional function, for whatever reason, proved to be especially popular in Revolutionary War monuments.

Funerary columns embracing a range of shapes, sizes, types, and styles were often placed atop graves, as the versatility of Doric, Ionic, Corinthian, or Tuscan details provided traditional variety. Some column shafts were fluted; some were left smooth. Some, as we have noted, were tall and imposing, while others were rendered on a more human scale or were deliberately halved or broken, symbolizing melancholy ruin and untimely death. Although the funerary columns were usually not as large as the civic, public versions, upon occasion they, too, were towering in scale. One such example stands atop the Henry Clay mausoleum (Fig. 47) in the Lexington Cemetery, Lexington, Kentucky (this tomb, built 1857-61, is briefly discussed in the Egyptian revival section of this book because the burial vault was inspired by Egyptian elements).

Another example of an imposing column is found above the burial chamber of Stephen A. Douglas (see Fig. 48). Located on land originally owned by Douglas near the shores of Lake Michigan in Chicago, the monument was begun shortly after the 1861 death of the statesman who is today remembered primarily for his famous debates with Abraham Lincoln. In his time, Douglas was well known for his political activity in the Democratic Party and for his outspoken advocation of the westward expansion of the United States. In the presence of President Andrew Johnson, General Ulysses S. Grant, Admiral David G. Farragut, and other notable Americans, the cornerstone of the monument was laid on September 6, 1866. Though many years would pass before its completion and final dedication in 1881, the monument was well publicized throughout the entire process from conception to completion and probably encouraged a number of other, similar designs.[52] The basic scheme—a column topped by a figure, with the base ornamented by bronze bas-reliefs, and with figures seated or standing at the sides or corners of the base—can be readily seen in European predecessors. The type was popular during the Baroque period and continued to be used well into the nineteenth century. Indeed, a similar design dedicated to the Virgin Mary could be observed during its construction in Rome by the colony of American sculptors living and working there. The Column of the Immaculate Conception was erected in Rome in 1856, and the designer of the Douglas monument,

Leonard Wells Volk, who studied in Rome between 1855 and 1857, might well have admired this Italian model and reinterpreted the design to suit the function and iconography of Douglas' tomb.

The striking William Lytle monument (Fig. 49) in Cincinnati's Spring Grove Cemetery features a broken column entwined with laurel garland and topped with an eagle. The imagery on Lytle's monument pointedly refers to his military profession: a relief on the die of the base depicts the Civil War general leading his troops at Chickamauga, where he met his death. The original design was by Louis Verhagen, a Belgian-born sculptor who made New York his home, and the present monument is a 1915 granite reproduction of the marble original which had become badly weathered and deteriorated.

The column has been used as a public or civic monument to glorify the memory of political and military heroes since the time of the Romans, and it was popularly revived in the nineteenth century for

Fig. 47. Henry Clay column and mausoleum, Lexington Cemetery, Lexington, Kentucky. Photo by Richard E. Meyer.

this purpose in both Europe and America. In 1809, a petition was submitted to the Maryland General Assembly by a number of Baltimore citizens requesting permission to institute a public lottery to finance a monument to George Washington. The eventual result of this petition was an impressive column constructed between 1815, when the cornerstone was laid, and 1829, when the final portion of the figure of Washington was raised to the summit. The

Washington Monument in Baltimore (Fig. 50) was the first column of major proportions (it stands approximately 130 feet high) erected in the United States. It was designed by Robert Mills, who was awarded the commission following an 1813 design competition.[53] Mills tactfully emphasized his American heritage and native professional training in a written appeal to the judges. However, both the original drawing for the monument and the subsequent modifications lack the

Fig. 48. Illustration of Stephen A. Douglas Monument, Chicago. From *Harper's Weekly* (1864).

unique American ingenuity of design Mills seemed to promise in his abasement of foreign born or trained competitors. There were in fact many European precedents for the use of commemorative columns. Sir Christopher Wren's early design for a column dedicated to victims of the 1666 Great Fire of London was well known to Americans, while the most familiar European columns from the nineteenth century were the Colonne Vendôme in Paris (1810), the Nelson Columns in Dublin and Edinburgh (1805 and 1808), and the Nelson Column in Trafal-gar Square, London, which was erected in 1838 (i.e., after the Baltimore column). None of these European designs have the same weighty visual effect as the Baltimore column, which looks austere and bulky by comparison. Mill's earliest designs for the Baltimore monument, it is true, involved a plethora of American symbols and imagery. The final column, however, differs significantly from Mills' original plans: his earliest designs were frequently modified as lottery funds dwindled, and the profuse exterior ornamentation of the column submitted in the early study was stripped. Most of the decisions concerning these modifications were made by a board of managers who consulted with Mills, and the changes most certainly were the result of monetary constraints rather than aesthetic preference. Obvious compromises included the elimination of surface decorations and the six galleries around the column shaft, simplification of the foundation chamber, and a substitution for the top sculptural group. Instead of a grandiose quadriga, or victory charioteer, a Roman-dressed Washington, sculpted by Enrico Causici, tops the columns. Many of the same design modifications were to recur in Mills' 1833 plans for the Washington Monument in Washington, D.C.

Motivations for the construction of columns as memorials during this period may occasionally be gleaned from concomitant writings. Thus, a poem composed for the dedication of the Robert E. Lee Monument in New Orleans in 1884 indicates the sentiments behind its elevation as it begins:

Fig. 49. William Lytle monument, Spring Grove Cemetery, Cincinnati. Photo courtesy Spring Grove Cemetery.

> Rear aloft the solid column—
>   Rear it high that men may see
> How the valiant honor valor—
>   How the brave remember Lee.
> Poise him on the lofty summit
>   Of the white enduring stone,
> Where his form may linger, teaching
>   In dumb majesty along.[54]

The Lee column (Fig. 51), which is very similar to the 1855 Henry Clay memorial in Pottsville, Pennsylvania, was designed by a New Orleans engineer and architect, John Roy, while the sculpture of Lee atop the column was executed by Alexander Doyle, who was born in Ohio and educated both in America and at Florence and Carrara, Italy.

Although a number of American civic columns commemorated statesmen and historical figures, the majority were associated with

Fig. 50. George Washington Monument, Baltimore. Photo by Lightner Photography.

Fig. 51. Dedication ceremonies of the Robert E. Lee column in New Orleans, 1884. Photo courtesy Historic New Orleans Collection.

military monuments. The aftermath of the Civil War encouraged citizens to elevate numerous Army-Navy or Soldiers-Sailors monuments, and columns were a popular form commonly employed for this purpose. A standard design recurring in the 1870s and 1880s features a central column supporting a female figure that represents Peace, Victory, Liberty, the Union, or a "genius loci," and a base supporting either four figures that denote branches of the military service or allegories of virtues, victory, or defeat. The Civil War Memorial (also known as the Soldiers and Sailors Monument) designed by Martin Milmore and erected between 1870 and 1874 on the Boston Common represents this type (Fig. 52). James Jackson Jarvis in 1869 prophetically observed that "Soon there will be seen in high places and in low, huge effigies, in bronze and stone, of volunteers on guard, at corners of columns, obelisks, and shafts of every conceivable degree of disproportion, misapplication, and inappropriate ornamentation, dedicated to the heroes of our last contest."[55] Jarvis' prediction was as accurate as his description was unflattering: within a relatively short period of time these monuments were literally vulgarized by redundancy. Standardized monuments such as those Jarvis criticized conveniently met the needs of committees acting for the general public, and the symbolism must have been acceptably understood by most viewers. Some columns were constructed on battlefield cemeteries and battle sites; however, most of these military monuments were located in prominent urban locations and were a constant visual reminder of the sacrifices made by those who served in the war between the states and other wars.

Despite Jarvis' criticism of American artists—he stated that "the greatest number of our monuments have no unity of parts or purpose; are crude or commonplace in conception; either made up hastily for the market, or unadvisedly stolen or altered from preceding work"[56]—it was ultimately the public that approved of the monuments through selection committees. The monuments commonly conceived by artists or monument companies,

whatever their limitations in terms of originality, clearly suited public tastes and expectations. In addition to the most popular type, that is, the column with four figures at the base, other variations occurred with more or fewer figures added to the base and with the column or shaft raised, lowered, or decorated with patriotic symbols.[57]

Along with the column used in Civil War designs, many additional columnar monuments were erected during the centennial years of the American Revolution. But whereas the Civil War monuments were often motivated by feelings of loss, grief, and didactic moralizing, Revolutionary War monuments constructed during the nineteenth century centennial celebration of the American Revolution were triumphant material statements celebrating and narrating battles fought and victories won. Pride rather than sorrow was the driving emotion behind their erection. Like Roman trophy columns, many of the Revolutionary War monuments were placed on actual battle sites. They often shared some of the same imagery employed by their Civil War counterparts, most especially the use of the column elevating an allegorical figure. Scenes of Revolutionary War battles, however, replaced Civil War imagery, with the thirteen original colonies and General Washington often featured. Examples of distinctive Revolutionary War monuments which utilize the column format include the Monmouth Battle Monument, the Battle of Yorktown Monument, and the Trenton Battle Monument. Other types, especially those inspired by the obelisk form, are discussed in later sections of this study.

Exedras

The neoclassical exedra, traditionally a rectangular or semicircular niche with seats, encouraged interaction between environment, structure, sculpture, and people. John Francis Stanley observed in 1912 that the ancient Greeks employed the design because of its practical nature, which provided seats for individuals attending commemorative rituals for the dead, and because the configuration

Fig. 52. Soldiers and Sailors Monument, Boston. Photo by David Berman.

helped enclose or define a particular burial plot.[58] Like the Greeks, the Romans often built exedras along roadsides where funerary shrines were both accessible and readily observable. Additionally, the Romans frequently combined the configuration with an altar or table for burial feasts. Although this form was widely used in ancient times, its classical heritage was not always emphasized, and the type did not actually become popular until the late nineteenth century, when it was increasingly used for both funerary and non-funerary commemorative memorials. Stanley, in extolling the advantages of the exedra form, went on to note that "There is a charm and sense of fitness in the exedra which properly qualifies it for a commemorative purpose, and the fact that it is coming into more general use indicates an advance in this field of endeavor."[59] When placed outdoors, the exedra integrates easily into the environment, the benches inviting visitation and contemplation of the surroundings. This feature made the design especially appropriate for rural cemetery settings and for public parks. When used in cemeteries, the design often consists of a long marble bench, generally inscribed with a family name and usually elevated on a platform the width of the burial plot. Occasionally sculpted figures are seated on the bench to continually mourn or pay respect to the dead, and as such are clearly auxiliary to the basic structural design. In other instances, the exedra was more obviously designed to emphasize and integrate figures into its concept. Architectural elements, especially columns or an abbreviated peristyle, were also combined with the standard exedra format. When employed in parks or battlefields, the exedra frequently became a stage for sculptural narration, with the bench consequently relegated to a secondary feature.

The famous monument commissioned by Henry Adams for his wife, Marian, and located in Rock Creek Cemetery, Washington, D.C. (Fig. 53), was designed in 1891 by Stanford White in collaboration with the sculptor Augustus Saint-Gaudens. Saint-Gaudens' powerful bronze sculpture of a heavily draped, shrouded woman sits within a hexagonal enclosure opposite a long stone bench, inviting contemplation and visitation in the cemetery environment.[60] The overall design format illustrates one potential for the ideal integration of structure, sculpture, and environmental design and the rich possibilities that the exedra concept provides for interpretation.

Another creative adaptation of the form may be seen in the Melvin monument (Fig. 54), designed in 1909 and situated within Sleepy Hollow Cemetery, Concord, Massachusetts. In this instance, the sculptor, Daniel Chester French, created a solemn, shrouded female figure representing Mourning Victory on a monument for the three Melvin brothers who had died in the Civil War. The partially draped figure, an angel or Nike symbol, emerges from the central block of marble that looms over the inscription slabs for the three brothers. In this variation, the rectangular exedra becomes a stage on which the sculpted figure performs, with the foundation functioning as a burial receptacle, or, in this particular instance, a cenotaph.

The Fuller monument (Fig. 55) in Chicago's Oak Woods Cemetery combines the exedra with the pergola, a structure often placed within a garden with lattice roof supported by columns and with wooden joists to accommodate climbing vines and garden plants. The Fuller monument is a granite structure with stone benches within the post and lintel framework. Small pedimented square markers for the individual family members are placed along the front. The integration of the monument with the cemetery environment complements well the functional accommodation of mourners at the site. The unique weightiness of the granite cross beams are, appropriately enough, strongly reminiscent of steel girders (the Fuller family owned a steel construction company in Chicago).

In public commemorative monuments, the sculpted figure of the person honored usually takes the prominent central position in the exedra design. This is true, for instance, in both the Richard Morris Hunt memorial (Fig.

Fig. 53. Adams monument, Rock Creek Cemetery, Washington D.C. Photo courtesy Library of Congress.

Fig. 54. Melvin Monument, Sleepy Hollow Cemetery, Concord, Massachusetts. Photo by Peggy McDowell.

Fig. 55. Fuller monument, Oak Woods Cemetery, Chicago. Photo by Robert Wright.

56) in New York City's Central Park and the Admiral Farragut Monument (Fig. 57), also located in New York City. The Hunt monument, designed by Bruce Price and sculpted by Daniel Chester French, was erected in 1898 to honor Richard Morris Hunt (1827-1895), a respected architect who helped found the American Institute of Architects and served as its president. Trained in painting, sculpture, and architecture at the Ecole des Beaux-Arts in Paris, Hunt was instrumental in encouraging Beaux-Arts classicism in America. The classical features of the Central Park monument are thus quite in keeping with Hunt's own neoclassical eclectic stylistic tendencies. Standing on pedestals at either end of the curved Ionic colonnade are two bronze female figures representing, respectively, the studio arts and architecture. The figure on the left holds a sculptor's mallet and a painter's palette upon which rests a small Dionysus copied from the Parthenon pediment, while that on the right holds a miniature building meant to represent the Administration Building of the Chicago World's Fair, which Hunt had designed. On a pedestal in the center niche, framed by a garland, stands a portrait bust of the versatile artist-architect. The pedestal is inscribed with Hunt's name, the years of his birth and death, and dedication information. Additional inscribed information concerning Hunt's background is provided on the low slabs between the smooth shafts of the Ionic columns. The monument as a whole, which was commissioned by the Arts Society of New York, thus represents a didactic use of the exedra configuration in order to make a powerful statement in text, sculpture, and style about this admired individual.

The Farragut monument, unveiled in 1881, was designed by Stanford White in collaboration with Augustus Saint-Gaudens. This public memorial was designed as a narrative scheme, and its innovative use of inscription and figural imagery is in marked contrast to the restraint of the previously-discussed Adams monument, also created by the same team. Like the Hunt memorial, the Farragut monument was designed to inform visitors to its Madison Square location. Unlike the Hunt design, however, the Farragut composition is quite devoid of neoclassical reference, with the exception of the exedra configuration. The exedra base for the bronze figure was begun in 1876-77 with a cost of $2,500. Saint-Gaudens received the commission for the bronze figure in 1876 and worked on the figure of Admiral Farragut in both Rome and paris. A preview of the monument in *Scribner's Monthly* for June, 1881 complimented the genius of the design and expressed the desire that the monument mark "the beginning of an era when we shall no longer import for our streets and parks the work of second-rate European sculptors, nor put commissions into the hands of Americans who have no claim whatever to the title of sculptor."[61] David Glasgow Farragut (1801-1870) achieved fame as a naval commander who served in both the War of 1812 and the Civil War. Perhaps he is most famous today for his exclamation which is often popularly interpreted as "Damn the torpedoes, full speed ahead!" The admiral's efforts to secure Rebel coastal forts during the Civil War contributed greatly to the success of the Union campaigns. In his memorial, a full portrait figure of Farragut stands firmly atop a central pedestal, making the exedra an extended base for the sculpture. The exedra itself is adorned with relief and incised undulating lines that refer to the sea. Two female figures in low relief representing Loyalty and Courage flank the central plinth, and fish adorn the bench ends. Across the back of the exedra, between the fish and the female figures, the inscription dedicates the monument and provides information about the admiral's historical exploits.

In Vicksburg National Military Park, the striking Missouri Monument (Fig. 58) also refers to the sea, though in this instance the reference has its origin in the Hellenistic Greek Nike of Samonthrace. The central figure of a monumental winged Victory stands on the prow of a stone ship that emerges from the tall central slab of the exedra design. In relief on either side of the monumental stele-like central unit are dramatic figures of the

Fig. 56. Richard Morris Hunt Memorial, Central Park, New York City. Photo courtesy Art Commission, City of New York.

Fig. 57. Farragut Monument, New York City. Photo courtesy Art Commission, City of New York.

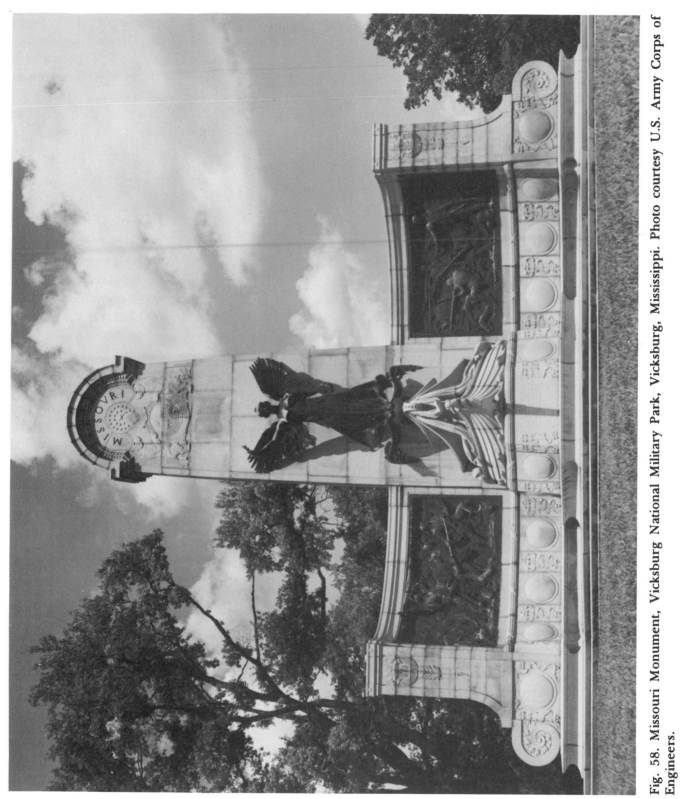

Fig. 58. Missouri Monument, Vicksburg National Military Park, Vicksburg, Mississippi. Photo courtesy U.S. Army Corps of Engineers.

Missouri troops at war on the Vicksburg battlefield. Designed by the firm of Helmuth and Helmuth and sculpted by Victor Holmes, the monument was dedicated in 1917. Unlike the type of exedra that invites the viewer to sit and contemplate, this monument is overtly and powerfully theatrical, and the visitor who sits on the benches may well feel overwhelmed by the sculptural performance.

The exedra was especially popular in military parks, and another variant can also be seen at Vicksburg. Near the Missouri memorial stands the Iowa Monument (Fig. 59), an interesting configuration which blends the exedra with an elliptical Doric peristyle. Although more architectural in nature and massive in scale in order to be impressive from a distance, the design nonetheless recalls in many respects the Hunt monument in New York City. Panels with relief sculpture depicting military conflicts are placed between the Doric columns, providing a dramatic narrative context similar to that afforded by the Missouri Monument. Henry H. Kitson was the designer, with additional collaboration from Mrs. T.A.R. Kitson in the creation of the equestrian figure. The monument was dedicated in 1906, with the equestrian figure added in 1912.[62]

Numerous other examples in cemeteries, cities, and rural battlefields attest to the popularity and versatility of the exedra, which was also included in mausoleum designs as a portion of the portico or within the interior as part of the sepulchral furniture.

Cemetery Entrances

Many nineteenth century cemetery entrances were inspired by classical as well as medieval and Egyptian revival sources. A nineteenth century lithograph of Philadelphia's Laurel Hill Cemetery (Fig. 60) depicts the classical style entrance and the picturesque landscape with trees, hills, and meandering roadways, all of which were conceived by John Notman circa 1836. The design of the entrance recalls the Greek stoa, which Notman modified into a colonnaded wall with a central office building. More recently, a photograph of the central portal entrance taken from inside the cemetery (Fig. 61) reveals that the nineteenth century entrance still functions as it was intended. The symmetry and horizontal stability of the structure contrasts sharply with the natural hilly environment that surrounds the portal and effectively works as an aesthetic complement, a propylaeum to the arcadian fields of the cemetery itself.

3. MEDIEVAL REVIVAL

In both nineteenth century literature and art, the middle ages were often equated with a period of spiritualism and chivalry, an era that inspired the finer nature of humankind. This romantic interpretation of medieval society was especially evinced in English novels and poetry, perhaps best epitomized in the works of Sir Walter Scott, which were read with escapist fervor by Europeans and Americans alike. In the latter half of the eighteenth century, Horace Walpole had encouraged the rebirth of the Gothic with his aristocratic connoisseurship of medieval architectural decorations and in his somewhat sensational novel, *The Castle of Otranto* (1765). John Ruskin's patronage of the Gothic architectural style in the nineteenth century further encouraged the popularity of medieval designs. His admiration of the purity of Gothicism, voiced by Augustus Welby Northmore Pugin before him, made the revival more acceptable and proper among learned Victorian theorists. Ruskin's *The Seven Lamps of Architecture*, published in 1849, was widely read and respected, as was his three-volume work, *The Stones of Venice* (1851-53). In mid-nineteenth century France, Eugene Emanual Viollet-le-Duc emerged as the major spokesman for the Gothic revival. In a number of volumes designed to both prove the rationalism of Gothic architectural principles and suggest the use of the Gothic for modern purposes, he vigorously defended the style, emphasizing its qualities over those of the Ecole des Beaux-Arts classical indoctrination.

The Gothic, or, as it is sometimes called, medieval movement was reborn as a result of popular interests in the romance of the period

Fig. 59. Iowa Monument, Vicksburg National Military Park, Vicksburg, Mississippi. Photo by Peggy McDowell.

Fig. 60. Illustration highlighting entrance to Laurel Hill Cemetery, Philadelphia. Photo courtesy Friends of Laurel Hill Cemetery.

Fig. 61. Interior view of entrance to Laurel Hill Cemetery, Philadelphia. Photo by Peggy McDowell.

and through ideological evaluation of the qualities, features, and potentials of the style associated with it. It was a self-conscious revival, with defenders that rivalled those pedantic academics of the classical revival school. By the late nineteenth century, a history of the movement, investigating both its inception and products, had already been published in England. Charles L. Eastlake's extensive *A History of the Gothic Revival* (1872) traces the origins of the use of medieval revival architecture in eighteenth and nineteenth century England and illustrates its contemporary applications, offering readers of his time an overview of nineteenth century positive as well as negative attitudes towards the style and defending its suitability in meeting current needs.

The major stylistic competitor of Gothic revival style was the classical revival, and contrasts were often drawn between the two. In America, Chester Hills argued in 1834 that "Although much has been said against this style of building...we find a lightness in Gothic designs and a boldness in their execution, which the Greeks and Romans never attained, or the moderns duly appreciated till within the last century. Formerly every design which did not perfectly accord with Grecian or Roman models was censured as barbarous and unworthy the attention of modern architects."[63] Hills continues in his introduction to Gothic principles of architecture by indicating that the English had studied the Gothic style and found it to be admirable and then utilizes material from the works of A.W.N. Pugin to provide examples for American builders. The fact that the models of the Gothic period had been studied and legitimized for modern use by English scholars would thus appear to have been extremely important in influencing American attitudes in this matter.

The controversy over the use of classical versus medieval sources actually became an emotionally charged issue on more than one occasion in England. When the British Houses of Parliament burned in 1834, the complex was rebuilt with the Gothic style dominating, though not without severe opposition by certain critics of medievalism. W.R. Hamilton, for one, associated the monuments of the middle ages with ideas of gloom, superstition, and barbarous extravagance, and he wrote vehemently against the use of the Gothic in the design for the seat of the legislative body of the United Kingdom.[64] Hamilton favored the classical revival and saw in classical art an expression of intellectual refinement, ideal beauty, and noble achievement, an argument which was countered by the point that classical revival design had its origins in heathen Greek times, while the English Gothic revival style was consistent with England's national heritage and spiritual character. The competition and motivations supporting classical versus Gothic styles often resulted in overly simplistic extremes of expression. The most often quoted was the intellectual approach associated with the classical contrasted with the spiritual motivations of the Gothic, or, as it was sometimes called, the Pointed Style. The association of the Gothic revival with the sentiments of Romanticism helped reinforce this view, though the fact that both the neoclassical and the Gothic could reflect the same Romantic spirit seems not to have been considered. Both styles were, in fact, quite popular in the commemorative arts, where association of the medieval with Christian doctrine and religious spirituality would certainly have helped support its growing use.

Along with the spiritual connotations of the style, Gothicism was frequently interpreted as a reflection of natural forms, an organic style in contrast to the geometric nature of the classical. Gothic revival designs thereby provided numerous aesthetic possibilities unrestricted by the analytical features of the antique classical traditions, and this potential was soon recognized by many inventive nineteenth century architects. It thus appears clear that a combination of both aesthetics and ideology helped make medieval revival forms popular and acceptable for a variety of uses, including their application to memorial art. A final appeal of the form was essentially practical in nature: Gothic revival features could be imposed with relative ease upon the most simple structure by the application of Gothic ornamentation and tracery.

American designers, who generally had not traveled to Europe to see Romanesque and Gothic architecture first hand, often depended upon published sources for their inspiration. Among the studies most frequently consulted were Batty and Thomas Langley's *Gothic Architecture Improved* (1742), Thomas Rickman's *An Attempt to Discriminate the Styles of English Architecture* (1819), and Augustus W.N. Pugin and T. Walker's two-volume *Examples of Gothic Architecture* (1831), all of which were published in England. American architectural guides and handbooks further served to illustrate specific details and plans for practical application of Gothic and other revival styles to contemporary buildings. Chester Hill's *The Builder's Guide* (1834), a work discussed earlier, included a special section on the Gothic using designs from A.W.N. Pugin for illustrations, and the style also received particular emphasis in David Henry Arnot's *Gothic Architecture Applied to Modern Residence* (1849) and Richard Upjohn's *Upjohn's Rural Architecture* (1852).

In the funerary arts, the Gothic and medieval world in general provided ample spiritual inspiration for designs based upon Christian traditions. The church iconographically was interpreted as Christ, a fitting symbolism that could be applied to a funerary structure. Burial within the church was a very old tradition which had often been reserved for the most influential parishioners, but by the nineteenth century anyone with sufficient funds could have constructed his or her own personal or family mausoleum as a replica of an *entire* church or chapel (and in contrast to neoclassical mausoleums, which usually emulated antique pagan temples). Medieval characteristics utilized in mausoleums ranged from Romanesque to various styles of Gothic, while scale moved along a continuum from modest, sparsely decorated simple church forms to large and flamboyant cathedral-styled structures. Other types of monuments inspired by the medieval revival include the ciborium or canopy design, with or without a spire, the Gothic aedicula, and the medieval altar or

funerary chest. Each of these had equivalent structures in the classical revival repertory of forms. Though the most obvious corollary existed between the temple and the church or chapel, both styles used the canopy, and the sarcophagus and table tomb could be interpreted with either classical or medieval features. Differences in the two styles were most often characterized by structural features, by surface decorations and patterns, or by both.

Canopies and Related Designs

One especially popular funerary monument was inspired by the Gothic canopy or ciborium. This configuration, as well as its neoclassical equivalent, has its origin in the Roman sacrarium. The hooded structure is frequently found over Gothic altars and tombs or sarcophagi. John Ruskin clearly expressed his appreciation of this type of monument in Volume I of his *The Stones of Venice*, wherein he described the tomb of Count Guglielma da Castelbarco (c. 1320) at St. Anastasia, Verona, a ciborium with Gothic canopy supported by four corner pillars, as a "pure and lovely monument, my most beloved throughout all the length and breadth of Italy—chief, as I think, among all the sepulchral marbles of a land of mourning."[65] An accompanying sketch verified its features.

One monument in particular that probably helped popularize the Gothic canopy design in the early nineteenth century was the tomb of Heloise and Abelard (Fig. 62), which was remodeled in the Gothic revival style when it was removed to Père Lachaise Cemetery around 1817-19. The effigies of the two ill-fated lovers rest atop sarcophagi ensconced beneath a Gothic canopy. The presence of their tomb within the new French cemetery further enhanced the prestige and popularity of the grounds: the monument was regularly visited by sightseers and romanticists, and contemporary illustrations of Père Lachaise almost always include reproductions of the structure. The tragedy of these lovers had been popularized a hundred years before in Alexander Pope's "Eloisa to Abelard," wherein the poet

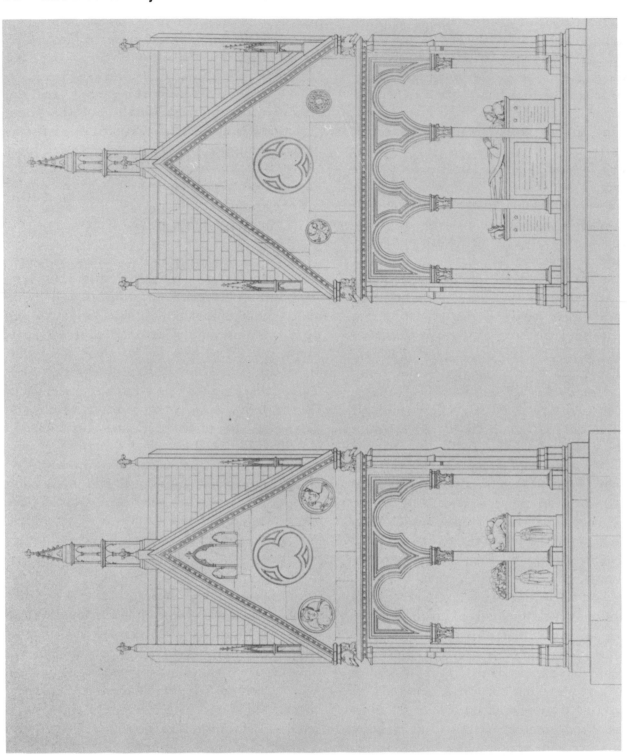

Fig. 62. Design of tomb of Heloise and Abelard, Père Lachaise Cemetery, Paris.

includes this reference to their death and burial: "May one kind grave unite each hapless name, / And graft my love immortal on their fame!" The stanza concludes, "Oh may we never love as these have lov'd!"[66] The associations of the monument with both spiritual and romantic love and with religion and death would most certainly have appealed to nineteenth century romantic temperaments and spurred its emulation in other funerary settings.

An obvious advantage enjoyed by this type of monument is its capacity to enshrine three-dimensional imagery. The enshrined object, usually visible through pointed arches, may be a standing or reclining figure, a sarcophagus, or some other form of symbolic image. The basic structure may be square or rectangular, and the scale may vary from small intimate designs to more massive structures which resemble displaced church spires. Because it enshrines utilizing forms associated with religious structures, the Gothic canopy, unlike its neoclassical counterpart, primarily connotes the spiritual ideals and moral virtues of the person commemorated. This association was probably the reason that the public memorial to Prince Albert, erected between 1863 and 1872 in London, emulated Gothic motifs and structural elements. A similar monument to Sir Walter Scott, designed in 1836 and constructed between 1840 and 1846 in Edinburgh, is a picturesque and florid interpretation of Gothic forms, perhaps implying in a somewhat theatrical manner the romantic drama as well as the religious values associated with the middle ages, the period that so fascinated Scott and his readers. Both these monuments employ Gothic canopies topped by towering spires.

The design that is most frequently employed within this general type is the canopy elevated above a square foundation with superstructure supported either by four corner columns, in the tradition of the ciborium, or by corner piers or buttresses. The canopy itself is more often a cross vault configuration than a dome. In the traditional square version, all four sides are the same, with repetitive features, thus ensuring balanced emphasis from all vantage points. An excellent example is afforded by the Martyrs' Monument in Trinity Churchyard, New York City (Fig. 63), commissioned by Trinity's vestry in 1852 at the request of the parishioners to commemorate the Revolutionary War dead, many of whom were buried in the churchyard. The identification of the structure with martyrs clearly recalls the martyrs of the early church and thus relates the commemorated dead to a saintly, or at least a sacred, sacrifice of life for a divine cause.

Variations on this primary configuration abound. The Firemen's Monument in Greenwood Cemetery, New Orleans, enshrines a sculpted and fully equipped figure of a fireman within the ciborium (Fig. 64). Dedicated to those firemen who had lost their lives in the line of duty and commissioned by the Firemen's Charitable Association, the memorial's design is similar, though not identical, to that of the Trinity Church Martyrs' monument, with pointed openings on four sides topped by pointed gables which are ornamented by foliated circles. The corners consist of buttressed piers, the buttresses decorated with small fleur-de-lis molding and flambeau crocket ornamentation on the spire. Built of Hollowell, Maine, granite in 1887, the monument was designed by Charles Orleans, who had lived for a brief time in New York City and might well have seen and been influenced by the Trinity monument. The sculpture of the enshrined fireman was modeled by Alexander Doyle and carved in Italy.

Human figures are not the only objects which may be thus enshrined. Beneath the sheltering spire of the Brown Family cenotaph in Brooklyn's Green-Wood Cemetery, a small sculpture of a ship foundering at sea refers to the 1854 disaster which took the lives of six family members (Fig. 65). In place of buttressed piers, columns support the structure and create a lightness of form. On close inspection, one finds the sculptural details to be creative interpretations of Gothic revival motifs, with lilies replacing the traditional fleur-de-lis or flambeau crockets.

Fig. 63. Martyrs' Monument, Trinity Churchyard, New York City. Photo by Peggy McDowell.

heart, with rude love of decorative accumulation: a magnificent enthusiasm, which feels as if it never could do enough to reach the fullest of its ideal."[67] Indeed, the monument is an appropriate illustration of variety, with little or no repetition or redundancy in sculptural details and decorative elements: even each of the gargoyles at the four corners is different. Both the Brown and Matthews monuments would appear to have been of interest to late nineteenth century visitors to Green-Wood, as they are illustrated in *Souvenir Green Wood Cemetery*, a small booklet of illustrations published in 1882 to accompany a tour of the grounds.

The same canopy configuration seen in the previous examples was modified by enclosing the space beneath the spire. Instead of the opening, stone tablets or plaques are framed by pointed arches on the four sides. The design is quite similar to the basic Gothic canopy; however, the enshrining function disappears, and the emphasis is upon mass rather than upon volume. Although it no longer contained canopy space beneath its spire, the Soldiers' Monument

The John Matthews monument (Fig. 66), also found in Green-Wood Cemetery, shelters two levels of figures under its Gothic vault. At the top, framed by the pointed arches, is a seated figure representing Matthews' wife, while on the bottom level reposes the gisant-like figure of Matthews himself. The monument is a feast to the eyes in its creative and personal translation of Gothic forms, bringing to mind the descriptions of the nature of Gothic as articulated by John Ruskin: "There are, however, far nobler interests mingling, in the Gothic

at Oberlin College, Oberlin, Ohio (Fig. 67), presented a design similar in its structural features to the Martyrs' Monument in New York City and the Fireman's Monument in New Orleans. Built in 1870 of Ohio sandstone and featuring marble inlays to commemorate the local men who died in the Civil War, many of whom were Oberlin College students, the principal design of the monument is credited to an Oberlin professor, Charles H. Churchill (his original ideas were elaborated upon by the firm of Heard and Blyth of Cleveland). Severe deterioration of the stone forced the removal of the monument in 1935.

Structures other than those elevated above the square foundation also traditionally enjoyed the function of enshrining or enclosing funerary imagery. In the middle ages, rectangular arcaded boxes with flat or gabled roofs often sheltered sarcophagi or reclining effigies; similarly, the Gothic parclose screened tombs within a sheltering enclosure. Both of the medieval funerary forms were revived for modern use in the nineteenth century. Two monuments in particular are noteworthy for the manner in which they employ ornate cuspate arches along the four sides of the rectangular enclosures. One of these, the monument to Mrs. George Leib Harrison in Philadelphia's Laurel Hill Cemetery (Fig. 68), is a quite delicate interpretation of the form. In a design attributed to John Notman, the intersecting arcade and the molding are enhanced by ornamental floral and leaf reliefs. A second example may be seen in the Pierrepont monument (Fig. 69), located in Green-Wood Cemetery, Brooklyn, and probably erected around 1860 (although

Fig. 64. Firemen's Monument, Greenwood Cemetery, New Orleans. Photo by Richard E. Meyer.

there is an earlier date on the inscription tablet, it predates the cemetery, with the next pertinent date being that of Anna Maria Pierrepont, who died in 1859). Henry Evelyn Pierrepont, one of the founders of Green-Wood, had been impressed with Richard Upjohn's interpretation of the Gothic style and commissioned him and his son, Richard Mitchell Upjohn, to design the Gothic revival gates for the cemetery (see Fig. 91), leading to the speculation that the Pierrepont monument either reflects the Upjohn influence or is, in fact, an actual design by the father or son.

Like the Brown and Matthews monuments discussed earlier, this tomb was reproduced in the 1882 carriage tour souvenir booklet for Green-Wood. A final example of this basic style is afforded by the A.C. Honore monument in Chicago's Graceland Cemetery (Fig. 70), which employs five cross-vaults to create a canopy above the burial vaults of the Honore family. The design is the product of the McKim, Mead, and White firm, and the monument was erected in 1905 at a cost of $18,100.

There are variations on the concept of the canopy used for sheltering a precious object.

Fig. 65. Brown Family cenotaph, Green-Wood Cemetery, Brooklyn, New York. Photo by Peggy McDowell.

Fig. 66. John Matthews monument, Green-Wood Cemetery, Brooklyn, New York. Photo by Peggy McDowell.

Fig. 67. Soldiers' Monument, Oberlin College, Oberlin, Ohio. Photo courtesy Oberlin College Archives.

Fig. 68. Mrs. George Leib Harrison monument, Laurel Hill Cemetery, Philadelphia. Photo by Peggy McDowell.

Fig. 69. Pierrepont monument, Green-Wood Cemetery, Brooklyn, New York. Photo by Peggy McDowell.

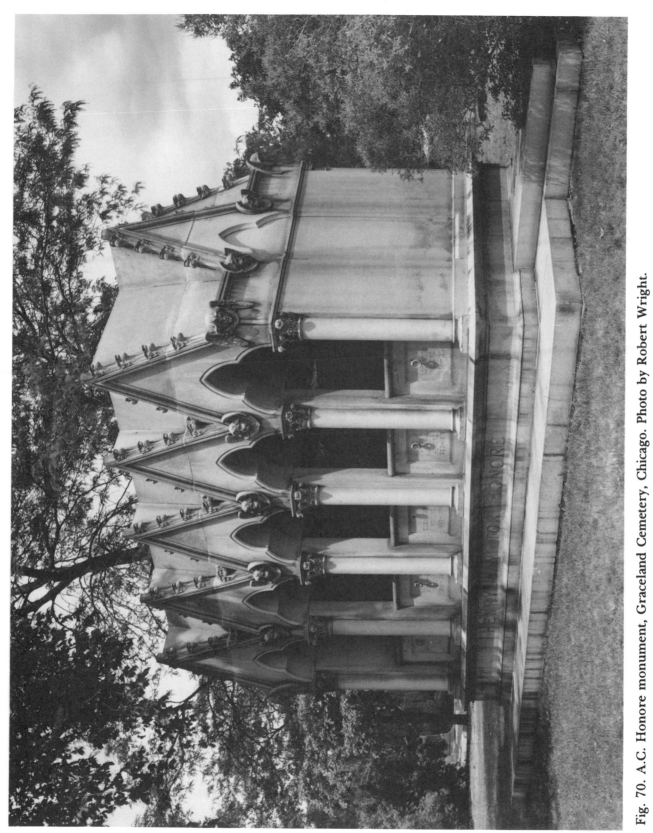

Fig. 70. A.C. Honore monument, Graceland Cemetery, Chicago. Photo by Robert Wright.

The aedicula, or canopied niche, for example, employed in the middle ages to enshrine a saint, altar, or relic, was also a type occasionally revived in the nineteenth century for funerary art designs. A splendid and somewhat famous example of a Gothic revival aedicula is the monument of Charlotte Canda in Brooklyn's Green-Wood Cemetery (Fig. 71). The basic design was supposedly sketched by the young Charlotte to mark the grave of her aunt, but ironically would come to be used for her own memorial. Within the niche, the figure representing Charlotte was carved by Robert E. Launitz and depicts her in the party dress she was wearing on the night she died. According to a contemporary review in *The American Architect and Building News*, this monument was frequently visited not only because of the impressiveness of its design, but also because of the tragedy that it represented, for, so we are told, "while returning from the festive enjoyments of a party of friends on the evening of her seventeenth birthday, February 3, 1845, Miss Canda was thrown from her carriage and almost instantly killed."[68] To many visitors to the site, Charlotte Canda's story, and by extension her monument with its highly personalized visual elements, thus typified the universal sadness occasioned by untimely death, a sentiment further reflected in a phrase of the poetic epitaph inscribed upon her memorial: "So fades—so falls—the opening rose, / Snapped, timelessly, before it blows."[69]

The monument of America's fifth President, James Monroe, is located in Hollywood Cemetery, Richmond, Virginia (Fig. 72), and consists of an intricate cast iron cage of Gothic tracery enclosing a marble sarcophagus, probably inspired by the Gothic parclose, a type of separating screen. It was designed by the architect Alfred Lybrock, a European who had immigrated to America and settled in Richmond. Monroe, a native of Virginia, died in New York in 1831 and was initially interred there. The Virginia General Assembly effected the transferral of the former President's remains to his home state in 1858, and the monument was erected over Monroe's grave shortly after his body was reinterred. The name and location of the manufacturers—Wood and Perot, Philadelphia—is cast in relief along the molding at one end of the frame. The skeletal tracery reminiscent of Gothic parclose design was particularly adaptable to cast iron because the material could duplicate the delicacy without sacrificing stability, though it does little to shelter the sarcophagus from the elements. Gothic design motifs of this type were also prevalent in iron fences and gates used in conjunction with cemetery plots. Although most effectively used with Gothic revival motifs, iron, it should be noted, was also employed for designs in classical revival styles.

Mausoleums

Along with creating delicate tracery patterns, iron was also recognized as a suitable building material for mausoleums. The mausoleum for the Edwards and Bennett families in Greenwood Cemetery, New Orleans (Fig. 73), is an example of such a cast iron fabrication and was probably erected in the 1860s. The choice of material seems especially appropriate in this instance as James D. Edwards and B.T.K. Bennett were foundry owners. Other cast iron tombs in this and neighboring cemeteries represent stock patterns duplicated and distributed throughout the United States during this period. One major problem that threatens iron is rust, and the material must be carefully primed and coated to stave off deterioration. John Jay Smith, in his 1846 publication, *Designs for Monuments and Mural Tablets Adapted to Rural Cemeteries and Church Yards*, quotes the secretary of Green-Wood Cemetery in Brooklyn on the proper care of iron railings, stating that "railings should be painted as soon as erected" and that at least three coats of paint should be applied with the base coat being a red lead pigment.[70]

The Edwards and Bennett mausoleum primarily depends upon surface ornamentation to identify the design with the Gothic. On the other hand, the J. M. Caballero tomb in St. Louis Cemetery II, New Orleans (Fig. 74), uses

Fig. 71. Charlotte Canda monument, Green-Wood Cemetery, Brooklyn, New York. Photo by Peggy McDowell.

Fig. 72. James Monroe monument, Hollywood Cemetery, Richmond, Virginia. Photo by Peggy McDowell.

Fig. 73. Edwards and Bennett Families mausoleum, Greenwood Cemetery, New Orleans. Photo by Peggy McDowell.

Fig. 74. J.M. Caballero tomb, St. Louis Cemetery II, New Orleans. Photo by Peggy McDowell.

both architectural and ornamental features to relate the design to Gothic sources. This marble mausoleum was designed in 1860 by J.N.B. de Pouilly and is the most ornate tomb constructed from the architect's repertory. Though the architectural element immediately recalls the Gothic, the effect of the surface details dominates the structure, imparting to the whole a delicate elegance much like that found in a medieval reliquary chest.

Whereas the Edwards and Bennett families tomb, and to a major degree the Caballero mausoleum, focus on the ornamental character of the Gothic, the Dexter mausoleum in Cincinnati's Spring Grove Cemetery (Fig. 75) clearly emphasizes Gothic structural features as the primary visual element. Here, the ornamental complements without ever threatening to overwhelm. An obvious quality of the Gothic—the vertical thrust of the architecture—is quite well demonstrated by the Dexter design. Classical revival designs are traditionally balanced between horizontal and vertical elements, while the Gothic usually gives the effect of defying gravity with an upwards, heavenly emphasis. The heavy use of stained glass windows adorning the walls recalls another traditional feature of the middle ages, though the use of stained glass was not necessarily limited to Gothic revival designs. This impressive cathedral-styled mausoleum, enriched with spires, tracery, and flying buttresses, was designed by a leading Cincinnati architect, James K. Wilson, and erected in 1869.

The Belmont mausoleum in Woodlawn Cemetery, the Bronx (Fig. 76), family tomb of Oliver Hazard Perry Belmont (1858-1908), illustrates the eclectic use of a specific late medieval prototype, the Chapel of St. Hubert at the Chateau de Amboise in the Loire River Valley of France, which was designed by Leonardo da Vinci and is said to house his remains (Fig. 77). The original design was translated for the use of Alva and Oliver Belmont by R.H. Hunt, who was following in the footsteps of his father, Richard Morris Hunt, as architect for the social elite. The delicate spire, ribbed vaulting, flamboyant decorations, gargoyles, and stained glass windows all

have marked precedence in French high Gothic architecture. The iconography of the fifteenth century chapel is also copied in the relief sculpture of its nineteenth century New York counterpart. Occupying the lintel above the main portals are relief figures of St. Hubert, patron saint of the chase, St. Anthony, St. Christopher, and in the center, surrounded by dogs, a stag with a cross between his antlers, the quarry that converted St. Hubert to Christianity. The Madonna and Child, flanked by the kneeling figures of Charles VIII of France and his queen, Anne of Brittany, dominate the tympanum. The symbolism of the stag is found again in a crown of antlers that encircles the base of the copper spire. The association of the Belmonts with the hunt and St. Hubert may refer to Oliver Belmont's love of horses as sporting animals. It is probable in any event that the couple wished to suggest their implicit alliance with the elements of aristocracy and genius investing the original source.

One of the most elaborate tombs in Woodlawn Cemetery (Fig. 78) is that of dry goods magnate John Harbeck (1839-1910). The design, conceived by Theodore E. Blake, is an eclectic assemblage that defies precise categorization. The relief panels around the octagonal exterior wall, the flying buttresses at the corners, the blind arcade incorporated into the clerestory exterior, the oblique point of the gable that frames the tympanum, and the heavy bronze doors decorated with relief sculpture all relate the design to medieval sources. The exterior is prolifically embellished with ornate finials and decorative reliefs, and the interior dome beneath the octagonal spire is covered by rich mosaics. The interior even features its own pipe organ. In its eclecticism, the plan parallels the centrally domed classical revival design and is reminiscent of "Gothick Temple" and "Umbrello" illustrations from Batty and Thomas Langley's *Gothic Architecture Improved* (1742).

Predictably, not all impressive mausoleum designs were original in their architectural and decorative features. Designs were often borrowed, and a similarity of mausoleum designs usually indicated a common source of inspiration or a stock pattern that could be personalized for individual use. As an example, the same centralized configuration—crossed gables with central tower—is repeated in a number of mausoleums in various locations. The Harrah mausoleum (Fig. 79), situated in West Laurel Hill Cemetery, Bala-cynwyd, Pennsylvania, was designed from an illustration, according to cemetery records. The date on the door is 1881. The Austell mausoleum (Fig. 80), Oakland Cemetery, Atlanta, Georgia, is similarly marked with the date (1883) cast on the lower door panels, while the Schmidt, Ziegler, and McStea mausoleums (Fig. 81) in New Orleans' Metairie Cemetery date from between 1885 and 1901. The striking similarities of all the mausoleums imply the use of a stock design that was repeated with some slight modifications, though the link or source that verifies the relationship is not

Fig. 75. Dexter mausoleum, Spring Grove Cemetery, Cincinnati. Photo courtesy Spring Grove Cemetery.

documented. The New Orleans versions were built next to each other by Charles Orleans, an agent for the Hinsdale Granite Company of New York, and the stylistic relationship of the three tombs is made even more apparent by their proximity. In what constitutes the slightest of variations, the Schmidt mausoleum (the tomb on the far left in Fig. 81) employs round instead of pointed arches on its four sides, and

the octagonal lantern cupola has been replaced by a dome.

The Richards mausoleum (Fig. 82) in Atlanta's Oakland Cemetery features a relatively restrained interpretation of medieval structural features. The slight hint of the pointed arch, the weighty square tower surmounted by a spire, the small windows, and the rustication of the stonework actually refer the design to Romanesque and early Gothic

Fig. 76. Belmont mausoleum, Woodlawn Cemetery, the Bronx, New York. Photo by Peggy McDowell.

sources. The Richards tomb is signed H.Q. French, New York, and was probably constructed in the late nineteenth century (i.e., 1885-90). The Joseph A. Walker mausoleum (Fig. 83) in Metairie Cemetery, New Orleans, also refers to Romanesque sturdiness, with the design emphasizing the fortress-like security of weighty stone sheltering and protecting the contents. The surface is enriched by the contrasting textures and colors of the granite from which the tomb was constructed. Evidence suggests that this monument was probably built by Charles Orleans in the late nineteenth century.

A castle-like weightiness is also evident in the James A. Garfield mausoleum in Cleveland, Ohio (Fig. 84). President Garfield died as the result of an assassin's bullet on September 19, 1881. During the eighty days that Garfield clung to life after being shot by Charles Guiteau, a politically disgruntled malcontent, the country reflected on the tragedy and prayed for the newly elected President. His death was an

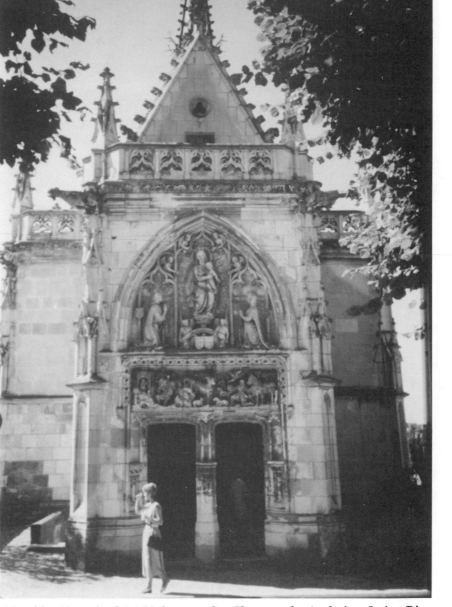

Fig. 77. Chapel of St. Hubert at the Chateau de Amboise, Loire River Valley, France. Photo by Jean Cramner.

emotional and political tragedy for a nation still trying to recover from the turmoil caused by the Civil War and Reconstruction. Disregarding personal political affiliations, a unified nation contributed to the construction of a monument deemed worthy of a martyred President. Garfield, a native of and former Senator from Ohio, was returned to his home state for burial, and his mausoleum was erected in 1890 in Cleveland's Lakeview Cemetery. Funds were raised by the Garfield National Monument Association, which also held an open competition for tomb designs won by George Keller of Hartford, Connecticut in 1884. Keller was assisted by John S. Chappel from London, who supervised the rich interior ornamentations. A massive three-stage circular tower, 150 feet high and fifty feet in diameter, dominates the structure, which is constructed of Ohio sandstone laid in random coursed ashlar. A rectangular vestibule functions as a narthex into

Fig. 78. Harbeck mausoleum, Woodlawn Cemetery, the Bronx, New York. Photo by Peggy McDowell.

Fig. 79. Harrah mausoleum, West Laurel Hill Cemetery, Bala-cynwyd, Pennsylvania. Photo by Peggy McDowell.

Fig. 80. Austell Mausoleum, Oakland Cemetery, Atlanta. Photo by Peggy McDowell.

Fig. 81. Schmidt, Ziegler, and McStea Families mausoleums, Metairie Cemetery, New Orleans. Photo by Warren Gravois.

Fig. 82. Richards mausoleum, Oakland Cemetery, Atlanta. Photo by Peggy McDowell.

Fig. 83. Joseph A. Walker mausoleum, Metairie Cemetery, New Orleans. Photo by Peggy McDowell.

Fig. 84. James A. Garfield mausoleum, Cleveland. Photo by Martin Linsey.

the circular chapel, the main floor of which contains a sculpture of Garfield standing before his congressional chair (Fig. 85). Beneath this floor is the crypt for the President and his wife. The exterior of the narthex is enhanced by a triple arcade with central portal inspired by medieval church facades. Across the top, relief panels carved in life-size scale by Casper Buberl represent Garfield as teacher, statesman, soldier, President at his inauguration, and martyred President lying in state. The effect of the interior, profusely decorated with polished granite, marbles, golden mosaics, and stained glass windows, resembles a combination of Byzantine and Gothic grandeur in the tradition of Victorian Gothic. The mausoleum became a nineteenth century version of a martyrium and remains open to visitors today. Here, instead of referring to the grandeur of the ancient Greek and Roman statesmen and their tombs, as is often the case in the grand monuments to American Presidents, the architect, quite possibly in consideration of the circumstances surrounding Garfield's death, drew from the Christian tradition of medieval martyriums enshrining relics of the saintly devout.

Altar Tombs, Mock Ruins, Gates, and Towers

Ornamental tracery and decorations from medieval sources, when applied to plain surfaces, could transform the tombstone, square pedestal, rectangular table tomb, or sarcophagus into a Romanesque or Gothic design. For example, the John Cornell monument (Fig. 86) in Green-Wood Cemetery, Brooklyn, is described by Nehemiah Cleveland in his 1857 directory for visitors to Green-Wood as an altar tomb, a term defined and illustrated (Fig, 87) in one late nineteenth century architectural glossary as "a raised monument resembling a solid altar."[71] As one may see by comparing the two illustrations, the tops of such monuments were traditionally flat, whereas the Cornell version is innovative in providing a low hipped roof with elevated pointed arches and finials at either end.

The inscription, in ornate English letters, indicates the monument was erected by the widow of John Cornell in 1848. It is constructed of freestone and was designed by J.C. Wells.[72]

Another characteristic sometimes associated with medieval revival architecture was the evocation of the picturesque and romantic atmosphere linked to the sublime grandeur of a decaying and solemn age long past. Gothicized funerary architecture would occasionally embrace this trend as well: the Bentinck Egan monument, for example, located in Metairie Cemetery, New Orleans, was built in the late nineteenth century as a "Gothick" sham ruins (Fig. 88). Great care was taken to carve irregularities such as cracks, weathering, and aging effects into the granite, and the passage of time has, in this instance, actually enhanced the charm of this miniature ruined chapel. Another instance of this phenomenon may be seen in the entrance to Hollywood Cemetery, Richmond, Virginia, which was constructed in 1876 in the form of a ruined tower (see Fig. 89). Members of the Hollywood Cemetery Company later decided to modify and expand the original design, credited to Henry Exall, to include the company office, temporary receiving vaults, and a small chapel. In 1897, the original "ruins" were completed to form a crenelated tower based upon a design by Marion J. Dimmock.[73]

Ruined or whole, the Gothic proved a popular model in the design of nineteenth century cemetery gates. The entrance gate to Chicago's Rosehill Cemetery, for instance, designed in 1864 by William W. Boyington, emphasizes the medieval castellated wall with crenelations, turrets, and rustic quarry-faced random range ashlar stone (Fig. 90). Its weightiness, quite in contrast to the original pseudo-ruins entrance of Hollywood Cemetery, would seem to more obviously imply protection and resistance to deterioration. Nonetheless, each in their own way, the Hollywood Cemetery and Rosehill Cemetery gates referred to the sheltering security associated with picturesque medieval walls and castles. Other cemetery gates emphasized the high Gothic lightness of the medieval church.

Fig. 85. Interior view of Garfield mausoleum, Cleveland. Photo by Martin Linsey.

Fig. 86. John Cornell monument, Green-Wood Cemetery, Brooklyn, New York. Photo by Peggy McDowell.

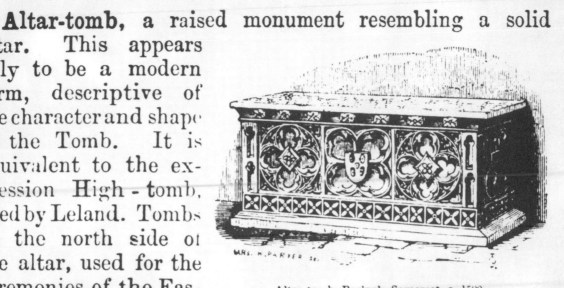

Altar-tomb—Ambo. II

Altar-tomb, a raised monument resembling a solid altar. This appears only to be a modern term, descriptive of the character and shape of the Tomb. It is equivalent to the expression High - tomb, used by Leland. Tombs on the north side of the altar, used for the ceremonies of the Easter *Sepulchre* were of this character.

Altar-tomb, Porlock, Somerset, c. 1500.

Fig. 87. Illustration, with definition, of an "altar tomb," from *A Concise Glossary of Architecture* (1888).

Inevitably, the use of Gothic revival designs for entrance gates also suggests the original use of churchyard burial grounds and the relationship of these grounds to the Christian faith.[74] When the rural cemeteries of the nineteenth century were constructed away from the churches, the reference to the church and the idea of sacred burial grounds could still be maintained indirectly through the design of the gates. When the dramatic verticality of pointed arches and spiked towers dominated, as in the Green-Wood Cemetery gates in Brooklyn (Fig. 91) and the gates to Crown Hill Cemetery in Indianapolis (Fig. 92), the lift of the visitors' eyes and senses to the heavens was an added spiritual sensation. The Green-Wood entrance gate was built in 1861 of Belleville brownstone from a design by Richard Upjohn in collaboration with his son, Richard Mitchell Upjohn. The tympanum reliefs above each portal were the work of John M. Moffitt. Adolph Scherrer designed the Crown Hill Cemetery entrance gates in 1885.

For compact vertical height, the medieval revival equivalent of the neoclassical column and the Egyptian obelisk was the crenelated circular tower. The tower was never as popular as the column or obelisk, however, and it was seldom used as a funerary monument. More often, it was erected as a marker on Civil War battlefields and occasionally as an historical commemorative monument. The Miles Standish monument in Duxbury, Massachusetts (Fig. 93) is an impressive example of this type. Standish, military leader of the *Mayflower* Pilgrim colonists, had later founded the town of Duxbury and died there in 1656. Creation of his memorial was sponsored by the Standish Monument Association, with Alden Frink serving as the architect. According to information published in 1900, the tower was constructed between 1872 and 1879 and reaches the height of 116 feet.[75] The monument, formed of rusticated granite, elevates a figure of Standish to a position high above the surrounding landscape. In 1898, an interior iron stairway was added, providing access to an observation room near the top from which visitors could gaze out and admire the sweeping view. A contemporary article in *Harper's New Monthly Magazine* illustrates the design as being located upon the flat shoreline of Plymouth Bay.[76] The monument, with its cylindrical sturdiness, resembles a lighthouse in this context. Although it was not actually built on the immediate shoreline, but rather upon a nearby hill, it did serve as a marker that could be viewed from both shore and sea. In his series of articles on "Early Settler Memorials," published in 1886-1887, T.H. Bartlett was not at all complimentary of the Standish monument, likening it to a large pepper box without artistic merit.[77]

The John T. Wilder monument (Fig. 94), erected between 1892 and 1902 on the Chickamauga Battlefield in Georgia, is similar in its features to the Standish tower. However, it was not used to elevate a sculpture. According to data furnished by the Chickamauga and Chattanooga National Military Park, it is constructed of local limestone and stands eighty-six feet in height. Although there are obvious visual associations with other objects, including the rook in traditional chess piece design, the lighthouse, and the pepper grinder, the crenelated tower design is historically associated with medieval castles, thereby connoting a fortress-like stability that was especially applicable to battlefield monuments.

Fig. 88. Bentinck Egan monument, Metaine Cemetery, New Orleans. Photo by Richard E. Meyer.

4. EGYPTIAN AND NEAR EASTERN REVIVAL

In Thomas Cole's painting, "The Architect's Dream" (1840), the artist features classical and Gothic structures in the foreground, while the Egyptian forms are placed in the background.[78] This would appear to be no accident, for it reflects in large measure an accurate placement of these styles in terms of their relative popularity in nineteenth cen-

Fig. 89. Illustration of original entrance to Hollywood Cemetery, Richmond, Virginia. Photo courtesy Hollywood Cemetery.

Fig. 90. Entrance to Rosehill Cemetery, Chicago. Photo by Robert Wright.

Fig. 91. Entrance to Green-Wood Cemetery, Brooklyn, New York. Photo by Peggy McDowell.

Fig. 92. Entrance to Crown Hill Cemetery, Indianapolis. Photo by Robert Wright.

Fig. 93. Miles Standish Monument, Duxbury, Massachusetts. Photo by Norman R. Forgit.

tury America. The Egyptian revival was often regarded with mixed feelings by European and American architects. Whereas the classical and Gothic revival styles each had their strong proponents who published studies, treatises, and profusely illustrated volumes supporting the use of those styles, the Egyptian revival did not enjoy such advantages. Consequently, Egyptian forms, at worst, were considered unfit, somber, and awful by some, while at best, other and less pedantic architects seemed to recognize the exotic potentials inherent within the grandeur and mystery of the style. For purposes of convenience, the Egyptian revival is often grouped with Near and even Far Eastern Oriental forms as constituting a loosely-related set of alternatives to the more traditional and seemingly repetitious European styles.

The Romans were the first culture to systematically introduce Egyptian fashion, religion, and art into Europe, and thereafter Egyptian objects were regularly incorporated into European design. In the eighteenth century, Piranesi proved to be particularly interested in Egyptianism. In one of his earliest publications, *Prima Parte di Architetture e Prospettive* (1743), the young artist illustrated a Roman "Burial Chamber" with pyramid and sphinx, and in 1760 he designed decorative walls using Egyptian motifs for the Caffe degli Inglesi near

Fig. 94. John T. Wilder monument, Chickamauga and Chattanooga National Military Park, Georgia. Photo courtesy National Park Service, U.S. Department of the Interior.

the Spanish Steps in Rome. These "English Coffeehouse" designs, along with other Egyptian-inspired motifs, were illustrated in his *Diverse Maniere*, published in 1769. Piranesi's imaginative use of Egyptian-inspired fantasy was extended to fireplace designs in this series, which concentrated on ornamental and decorative designs and accessories. There was even a minor trend in the eighteenth century to adapt

Egyptian motifs to the fanciful decorations of the Rococo. And the decorative and ornamental possibilities inspired by Egyptian design certainly did not go unnoticed by revival style designers of monuments during this period. Along with the more obvious architectural and structural features, many monuments included Egyptianized accessories such as doors, gates, fence panels, and posts.

Although there were various studies made of Egypt previous to the late eighteenth century, it was really the Napoleonic expedition to Egypt in 1798-99 that gave the major impetus to Egyptianism, and the first comprehensive publications signalling the onset of the movement resulted from this campaign. One of the earliest of these, a three-volume work by Dominique Vivant Denon entitled *Voyages dans la Basse et la Haute Égypte pedant les campagnes du General Bonaparte*, was published in 1802. Additionally, by order from Napoleon himself, there appeared between 1809 and 1828 a series of twenty-one volumes bearing the collective title *Description de l'Égypte ou Recueil des recherches qui ont été faites en Égypte pedant l'expedition de l'armée française* (See Fig. 95).[79] These volumes, which contained numerous large folio-sized drawings of Egyptian temples, reliefs, ornaments, tombs, and maps, were directly based upon observations and research done in Egypt during the expedition of the French army. Curiosity and interest aroused by the Napoleonic campaigns into Egypt encouraged travelers and explorers to visit, investigate, and describe the country. Architectural guidebooks, which before the late eighteenth century concentrated on classical and Gothic styles, began to include Egyptian and occasionally other "Oriental" styles as well, and the more versatile and flexible architects on both sides of the Atlantic soon incorporated Egyptian revival art into their repertoire.

Despite the fact that the Egyptian revival did not offer the Gothic and classical revivals much competition as a design inspiration for public buildings and private homes, it nonetheless found an important place in the nineteenth century commemorative arts. Perhaps because of the preponderance of Egyptian tombs and their furnishings, people seemed to naturally associate the civilization with death and funerary imagery. Furthermore, the religion systems of the Egyptians stressed the concepts of immortality, rebirth, and life after death of the body, ideas that were eminently compatible with Christian beliefs. The connotations of Egyptian timelessness and permanence were yet another factor favorable to funerary designs based upon such models. John Haviland, in his early nineteenth century *Practical Builder's Assistant*, captured many of these sentiments in observing that "the general appearance of the Egyptian style of architecture is that of solemn grandeur amounting sometimes to sepulchral gloom. For this reason it is appropriate for cemeteries, prisons, & c.; and being adopted for these purposes, it is gradually gaining favor."[80]

Obelisks

The obelisk is without question the most prevalent Egyptian form to be used in American funerary and commemorative art. In fact, owing to the manner in which it penetrated in vast numbers to even the humbler forms of cemetery monuments, it could—in this sense at least—lay claim to being the most pervasive of all the revival forms. Because it was so frequently employed in various materials and sizes, however, it ultimately lost the greater part of its Egyptian associations. Hardly ever a monolith, the nineteenth century obelisk was principally recognized for its potential of achieving great height atop a limited ground space, and height would definitely seem to have been a primary objective of some monument committees. Although not always a priority aspect in purely funerary designs or in monuments that were intended to commemorate the memories of those who had recently died, height became far more significant when the monument was meant to be enjoyed by the public as part of the celebrated commemoration of past heroes and victories. Such obelisks, like comparable columns and towers in the classical and Gothic modes, were often hollow, with stairs

Fig. 95. Illustration from *Description de l'Égypte....*

or elevators that led to a top viewing area. This may be seen, for example, in the diagram of the Bunker Hill Monument (Fig. 96), located in the Charlestown area of greater Boston, which lists the monument's height at approximately 220 feet. Though this is certainly impressive, other commemorative obelisks, such as the Bennington Battle Monument in Vermont (306 feet) and the famous Washington Monument in Washington, D.C. (555 feet), demonstrate even more dramatically the potential of this form for achieving great height and vertical thrust. All of these monuments provide access to the top for viewing and are in some fashion associated with American victory in the Revolutionary War or with the man who provided the principal American military leadership in that conflict.

The first obelisk design to be used as a monument in America is a brick construction erected in 1792 by the French consul on his estate in Baltimore (Fig. 97). This simple design with its tall, thin shaft was elevated to commemorate Christopher Columbus upon the tricentennial celebration of his historic voyage to America. Almost from its inception, however, the relative merits or demerits of the obelisk as a design form would become the basis for ongoing debates amongst critics and others. It was the stable, solid quality and the austere purity of line and surface which above all else made the obelisk appealing to designers. Unsympathetic critics of the obelisk, however, would undoubtedly have agreed with the rather harsh pronouncements of T.H. Bartlett. "An obelisk," he notes, "no matter how well made,

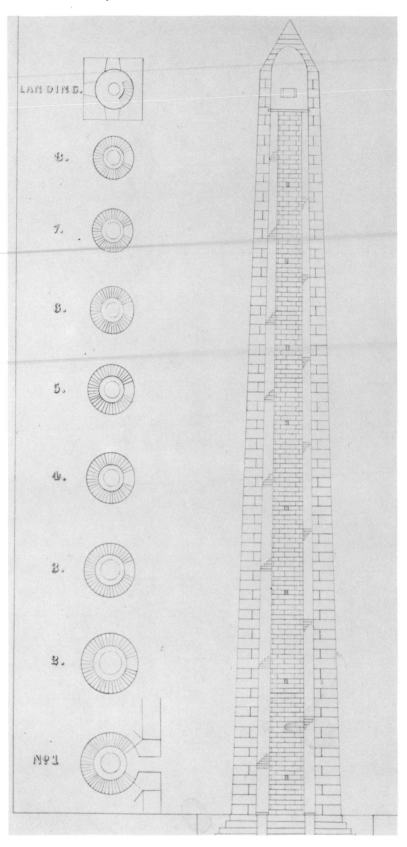

Fig. 96. Diagram of the Bunker Hill Monument, Charlestown Massachusetts.

Fig. 97. Columbus Monument, Baltimore. Photo by Harold Allen.

has never had any human interest as a memorial of the dead. It has, however, a universal interest peculiar to its origin and purpose. Its form, according to modern interpretation is the easiest and cheapest for grave-yard purposes, a convenient excuse for want of thought and an accepted apology for ignorance. A large obelisk is an excellent and popular means of gratifying vanity." The author continues by indicating contemptuously that it was "the form that could be built to the greatest height for the smallest sum of money."[81] While it seems doubtful that those people who built or commissioned obelisks as monuments were as egotistical or ignorant of style as Mr. Bartlett apparently believed, this critic was generally economical in his praise of style or design, and he was in any event one of the few writers of such articles in the last century who evaluated monuments in terms of artistic merits rather than historical significance. By the late nineteenth century, when Bartlett made these remarks, so many obelisks in every conceivable size and proportion had been constructed that the author was probably totally bored with the sheer and seemingly endless redundancy of the form. There was even by this time an alphabet block stacking toy, approximately three feet tall and patented in 1882, that described the history of Cleopatra's Needle, the obelisk given to the United States by the Khedive of Egypt in 1879 and erected in New York City.

Perhaps the most extensive criticism of the obelisk was voiced by opponents of the design for the monument erected in Washington, D.C. in honor of the nation's first President (see Fig. 98). Henry Van Brunt, writing for *The American Art Review* in 1880, was particularly critical of the obelisk designed by Robert Mills, stating that "the original design was conceived at a time when artistic education in America had not been begun," and likening the monument to a "dumb colossal chimney."[82]

Despite the verbal efforts of its detractors, there were in fact many proponents of the obelisk as well, and a number of prominent designers such as Benjamin Latrobe, Robert Mills, Horatio Greenough, Solomon Willard, Minard Lafever, and Thomas Jefferson utilized the form. Like the classical column, the obelisk was extremely versatile: it could easily be modified in scale from a small solid shaft atop a cemetery monument to a large hollow structure with or without interior stairs. However, the monumental obelisk offered an element of simplicity which the column with its classical details usually did not afford. The column most generally stopped the movement of the eye at the capital or at the figure on top, while the obelisk kept the eye traveling upward in a sweeping, dynamic movement, thereby reinforcing the essential verticality and effect of height. Perhaps because of this factor as much as anything else, there always seemed to be a healthy rivalry amongst builders of the larger obelisks to see who could achieve the greatest heights.

Probably the most famous testimonial to the obelisk was provided by Thomas Jefferson, who at one point wrote: "Could the dead feel any interest in monuments or other remembrance of them, when, as Anacreon says, 'we shall lie a little dust, the bones having been loosed,' the following would be to my manes the most gratifying: on the grave a plain die or cube three feet square, without any mouldings, surmounted by an obelisk six feet in height, each of simple stone."[83] Although Jefferson had also expressed an earlier interest in a Gothic funerary chapel for his grave, his preference for a simple obelisk gravemarker is made amply clear in this later statement. The monument was erected according to Jefferson's wishes in 1833 at his plantation, Monticello, near Charlottesville, Virginia, but soon both it and the inscription slabs covering the graves of the President and his family were badly damaged by souvenir hunters, whose methods extended to the use of sledge hammers in order to chip off pieces of the stone. Even a nine-foot brick wall with an iron gate, erected in 1837, did not prove sufficient to deter these dedicated relic seekers. In 1882, a member of Congress visited the gravesite and found it in such deplorable condition that he introduced a bill appropriating $10,000 to rehabilitate the site. Thomas L. Casey of the U.S. Army Corps

Fig. 98. Certificate of the Washington National Monument Society, illustrating designs of the Washington Monument and tomb. Photo courtesy Library of Congress.

of Engineers, the individual who also supervised the final construction phase of the Washington Monument in the nation's capitol, was given the responsibility for renovating Jefferson's grave. A new obelisk (Fig. 99) was elevated, with an enlargement of the original dimensions (though only a few inches larger at the base, the height of the replacement was increased to almost thirteen feet). The resulting visual effect is striking different: the later version is less chunky and proportionally resembles the true Egyptian obelisk in a rather more convincing fashion. Through a fortunate series of circumstances, the original monument was saved from destruction. Faculty of the University of Missouri, the first state university founded in the new territory created by the Louisiana Purchase, felt especially indebted to the former President for his role in negotiating the Purchase, and accordingly requested of Jefferson's descendants that the old monument be saved and placed on their campus. Their wish was subsequently granted, and the original marker was officially presented to the university in 1893.

In nineteenth century cemetery settings, the obelisk elevated by a square pedestal was a monument type erected with great frequency and on a scale ranging from modest to grand. The Donaldson monument (Fig. 100) in Laurel Hill Cemetery, Philadelphia, and the Shields monument (Fig. 101) in Brooklyn's Green-Wood Cemetery represent two contrasting interpretations of this configuration. These are roughly contemporaneous artifacts: the Donaldson monument is illustrated in the 1844 guidebook to Laurel Hill, and the Shields monument was designed by Minard Lafever and erected in 1845. Lafever used a rather idiosyncratic ornamental approach with the Shields design, in contrast to the more traditional Egyptian revival features exhibited in the Donaldson base and obelisk. In the latter instance, the pedestal, elevated by foundation plinths, employs the battered sloping shape, banded roll moldings at the corners and top, and cavetto Egyptian gorge cornice with winged disks—all typical features from Egyptian revival designs. The obelisk itself is without ornamentation. Lafever, on the other hand, indulged in sculptural decorations on all parts of the Shields monument, with bands of inverted lotus plants alternating on the shaft with banded roll moldings, and with another row of inverted lotus flowers decorating the base of the pedestal above an ornately inscribed battered plinth. A relief likeness of Ada Augusta, wife of Charles Shields, is prominently placed at the base of the obelisk above the die. The portrait bust itself is framed by short and long inverted lotuses. Lafever was obviously partial to this heavily decorative approach: he also proposed, in 1848, a similarly ornate obelisk on a grandiose scale for a monument to George Washington, which he illustrated in his study entitled *Architectural Instructor* (another sepulchral obelisk, also illustrated in the same volume, constitutes a variation on the Shields design).

In Springfield, Illinois, the tomb housing the remains of Abraham Lincoln, his wife, and three of their sons is surmounted by a 117-foot obelisk (Fig. 102). Following the President's assassination in April, 1865, a monument association was formed in Springfield to raise funds and supervise the monument during construction and after completion. In the customary manner, a competition was held to determine the best design, with the $1,000 prize going to Larkin Mead, an artist from Vermont. Mead's design concept consisted of a large ground-level mausoleum chamber topped by a tall obelisk supported on a base. On circular projections at the four corners of the base stand four separate groups of bronze figures designed by the artist. Like the figures found on many Civil War military monuments, these bronzes represent branches of the military, the "Defenders of the Union." At the center front there stands a large bronze figure of Lincoln. The tomb was formally dedicated in 1874, having taken more than four years to complete. Foundation damage necessitated a reconstruction of the tomb between 1899-1901, and the bodies were subsequently removed and reinterred in a crypt lying beneath the original burial chamber. A visitor to the site, Francis M. Palmer, writing in a November, 1901 article

Fig. 99. Thomas Jefferson Monument, Monticello, Virginia. Photo courtesy Jefferson Memorial Foundation, Inc.

Fig. 100. Donaldson monument, Laurel Hill Cemetery, Philadelphia. Photo by Harold Allen.

Fig. 101. Shields monument, Green-Wood Cemetery, Brooklyn, New York. Photo by Peggy McDowell.

Fig. 102. Tomb of Abraham Lincoln, Springfield, Illinois. Photo courtesy Department of Conservation, State of Illinois.

in *Munsey's Magazine*, noted that the recently renovated tomb had already been badly damaged by souvenir hunters. This ongoing vandalism quite possibly contributed to the need for a second major reconstruction, which took place in 1930-31. The access to the interior stairs through the base was sealed at this time by a large block of stone originally sent in 1865 by the citizens of Rome as a tribute to the fallen President (the block was taken from the wall of Servius Tullius, an Etruscan or Roman who, according to legend, was born a slave, became king, and died by assassination). The State of Illinois gained control of the site in 1895 when the last surviving member of the National Lincoln Monument Association deeded the property to the state.

Pyramids, Temples, and Other Inspirations

Predictably, the pyramid, probably the most well known of Egyptian funerary structures, was also a popular design in nineteenth century memorial art. Like the obelisk, the pyramid appears as a motif in Western art in various periods and in various manners before the nineteenth century. Precedence was not at all difficult to find, and nineteenth century designers used the forms in a variety of fashions within the funerary arts. In essence, the pyramid is a fundamentally simple structure and does not require any particularly special talents to build: elementary knowledge of construction techniques is the basic requirement.

The tomb of James Calhoun, early Mayor of Baltimore, is topped by a weighty pyramid (see Fig. 103, background), which illustrates this rather basic construction principle. The monument is attributed to Maximilian Godefroy and was erected in Baltimore's Westminster Cemetery sometime between 1813 and 1815. Godefroy is also credited with designing the neighboring Egyptian revival Robert and William Smith family tomb shown in the foreground of this illustration.

The stacking and layering of stone is clearly readable in most pyramidal designs, as evidenced in the mortared courses of similarly proportioned blocks of stone employed in the construction of the Calhoun tomb. Which is not to say that variety in visual effect was lacking. The Confederate Monument in Hollywood Cemetery, Richmond, Virginia (Fig. 104), while similar in overall configuration to the Calhoun tomb, achieves a strikingly different appearance through its use of stone that is more rustic and irregular. This monument, which stands approximately ninety feet in height and was erected in the Soldiers' Section of the cemetery in 1868-69, was designed by Charles H. Dimmock and was commissioned and funded by the Ladies of the Hollywood Memorial Association. It is constructed of James River granite blocks that are irregular and unevenly cut, many with drill holes clearly visible. This quality enhances its nature as a handcrafted work, much in the manner of early New England stone walls that were constructed without mortar. The result is an obvious primitive, picturesque quality which not only renders this work distinct and personal but also serves to reinforce the imposing presence of a monument dedicated to the Confederate dead.[84]

An impressive interpretation of the pyramid configuration utilized as a mausoleum became especially popular in the second half of the nineteenth century. Two remarkably similar examples, one in Illinois and the other in Louisiana, employ Egyptian portals flanked by female figures and sphinxes fronting monumental pyramids. While a construction date for the Schoenhofen mausoleum (Fig. 105), located in Chicago's Graceland Cemetery, cannot be precisely determined, drawings by architect Thomas Sully date the Brunswig mausoleum (Fig. 106) in Metairie Cemetery, New Orleans, to 1893. According to Metairie Cemetery sources, the Brunswig mausoleum was inspired by a funerary monument in Milan, Italy, leading to the inference that the prototype of the Schoenhofen design may have been the same or a closely related source.

In addition to its funerary and war memorial functions, the pyramid was also occasionally used as a marker to commemorate historical personages. Such is the case with a rusticated pyramidal monument (Fig. 107) designed

Fig. 103. James Calhoun tomb (background), Robert and William Smith tomb (foreground), Westminster Cemetery, Baltimore. Photo by Harold Allen.

Fig. 104. Confederate Monument, Hollywood Cemetery, Richmond, Virginia. Photo by Harold Allen.

Fig. 105. Schoenhofen mausoleum, Graceland Cemetery, Chicago. Photo by Harold Allen.

by Henry Hobson Richardson and erected near Laramie, Wyoming in honor of the Ames brothers, who became directors of the Union Pacific Railroad during the Lincoln administration and were instrumental in fostering the company's westward expansion. The location of the monument was set, appropriately enough, near a major mountain pass for the transcontinental rails.

Whereas the obelisk and pyramid appeared at various times before the eighteenth and nineteenth centuries, the tomb inspired by the Egyptian temple form was an innovative design. Designers of mausoleums borrowed from sundry Egyptian architectural features and ornamental motifs such as columns with papyrus bud, bell, and lotus capitals, walls with battered sides, cavetto cornices, and pylons. The winged disk, with or without serpent, was one of the most popular of all ornamental motifs.

Fig. 106. Brunswig mausoleum, Metairie Cemetery, New Orleans. Photo by Richard E. Meyer.

Two ornate versions of Egyptian temple mausoleums are illustrated in plate XVIII of John Jay Smith's 1846 work, *Designs for Monuments and Mural Tablets Adapted to Rural Cemeteries and Church Yards* (see Fig. 108). In his section on monuments, Smith states that his intent is "to give specimens of a variety of styles, and to insert nothing which in itself could be considered bad taste."[85] Quite obviously, the author's two illustrated "Egyptian Facades, For Vaults," which by his own definition must be in good taste, represent some rather garish alternatives for sculptural ornamentation based upon Mr. Smith's interpretations of the ancient temples of Osiris and Isis. Though not always with the extravagance demonstrated in the previous examples, mausoleums inspired by Egyptian temple prototypes were designed and constructed throughout the nineteenth and into the twenti-

Fig. 107. Ames Brothers Memorial, near Laramie, Wyoming. Photo courtesy Western History Research Center, University of Wyoming.

eth century as Egypt continued to be a popular destination for travelers, photographers, and explorers. Photographs of Egyptian sites were published in documentaries and travel books, as well as in newspapers and popular literature of all sorts. Typical of such efforts is the work of Francis Frith, whose photographs and descriptions of numerous Egyptian sites appeared in his aptly named *Egypt and Palestine, Photographed and Described*.[86] Volumes such as these offered architects, scholars, and the general public authentic contemporary views of these exotic sites instead of the line renderings or fantasies imagined by earlier designers, photographs provided more authentic contextual documentation. The spectacular discovery of the tomb of King Tutankhamen in 1922 encouraged a continuing interest in the Egyptian revival well into the third decade of the twentieth century.[87]

One persistent feature employed in revival designs based upon Egyptian temples and funerary structures is a cavetto cornice, often called an Egyptian gorge. This typical concave cornice was often decorated with vertical lines that referred to reeds, leaves, papyrus, or other vegetation, and was framed on the bottom by a roll molding. Such cornices usually topped the monument and were employed above the door or pylon posts. Another feature borrowed from

Fig. 108. Egyptian temple mausoleum designs: plate XVIII of *Designs for Monuments and Mural Tablets...* (1846).

Egyptian sources consisted of columns with bell capitals. The column shaft with its organic shape, like the capital, often referred to the papyrus plant. On the previously-discussed Robert and William Smith tomb design (see Fig. 103), the columns are engaged and flank the doors.

The Swaim monument (Fig. 109) in Philadelphia's Laurel Hill Cemetery uses all

Fig. 109. Swaim monument, Laurel Hill Cemetery, Philadelphia. Photo by Harold Allen.

the basic features of the Egyptian revival vocabulary in a miniature scale on a table tomb configuration, with hieroglyphs added to complete the Egyptian reference. The monument was commissioned by James Swaim upon the death of his father, William, in 1846, and the following year *The Philadelphia Public Ledger* described the tomb as surrounded by eight obelisks (no longer extant), "on which the name of the deceased is sculptured in Hieroglyphic characters." "This tomb," the article continues, "presents a novelty to the beholder, and the peculiarity of the style, with the emblems and designs upon it, carry the mind back to a people whose veneration and respect for their dead seem stronger than for the living."[88] The capitals of the engaged columns on the Swaim tomb are decorated with a date palm motif similar to that used by John Haviland in his design for the Pennsylvania Fire Insurance Building. The monument was carved by John Maples, and the name of the architect who designed it, Gordon Parker Cummings, is visible on one of its corners. William Swaim was well known for his nationally distributed patent medicine, "Swaim's Panacea," which supposedly provided relief from an array of maladies.

Along with the engaged column, such as seen on the Swaim table tomb and the Robert and William Smith tomb, other Egyptian revival columns function much like the classical column in antis. An early nineteenth century example of this concept is provided in the Ball Tomb (Fig. 110), also in Laurel Hill Cemetery, which was designed by Thomas U. Walter in the 1830s. Here, the facade presents slightly battered end walls and is built into the side of a hill, recalling the integration of architecture and landscape that is found in many Egyptian monuments dating from the Middle and New Kingdoms. The wide horizontal emphasis of Walter's design also serves to reinforce the landscape features of the site.[89]

The Johnston tomb (Fig. 111) in Brooklyn's Green-Wood Cemetery presents a facade framed by another feature typical of many Egyptian revival designs, roll moldings that are decorated with wrapped ribbon lineation (this design concept is often found in Egyptian revival source books of the period). The top of the portal of the tomb is decorated by the corbel configuration. The distinctive shape of the door is not as unique as it might at first appear: such openings were in fact often employed in Egyptian-inspired designs, one particularly impressive example being the lower level of the Egyptian Exhibition Hall in London, constructed in 1812.

The designer of the St. John mausoleum (Fig. 112) in the Grove Street Cemetery, New Haven, Connecticut, was especially sensitive to the complete ensemble of gate, gate posts, and tomb. The mausoleum door, however, with its Gothic wheel tracery, is a somewhat disturbing exception to the continuity of design. Repetitions of the winged orb, roll molding, and cavetto cornice with inscribed vertical bands are visible on the front pylon-like gate posts, cast iron fence, gate, and on the mausoleum itself. These motifs are similar to those found on the Grove Street Cemetery entrance (see Fig. 122 and discussion below).

The A. Grailhe Family mausoleum (Fig. 113) in St. Louis Cemetery II, New Orleans, was built in 1850 by stonemason P.H. Monsseau from the original design by architect J.N.B. de Pouilly. De Pouilly's sketchbook study of the tomb, now in the Historic New Orleans Collection, indicated even more ornamentation than that found on the constructed version. The ornamental details of tomb, doors, and fence design applied to this mausoleum, one of the earliest Egyptian revival tomb designs in New Orleans, are finely coordinated to produce continuity of design.

Somewhat by way of contrast to the simple elegance of the Grailhe monument, the weighty severity of the well-known Martin Ryerson granite mausoleum (Fig. 114), its battered walls that taper upward with a curving line, and the pyramidal reference of the hipped roof, all relate this design concept to the ancient Egyptian mastaba. This impressive structure, designed by the eminent Chicago architect Louis Sullivan in 1887, stands in that city's Graceland Cemetery.[90]

Fig. 111. Johnston tomb, Green-Wood Cemetery, Brooklyn, New York. Photo by Peggy McDowell.

Fig. 112. St. John mausoleum, Grove Street Cemetery, New Haven, Connecticut. Photo by Harold Allen.

Fig. 113. Grailhe mausoleum, St. Louis Cemetery II, New Orleans. Photo by Ralph Hogan.

Fig. 114. Martin Ryerson mausoleum, Graceland Cemetery, Chicago. Photo by Harold Allen.

Grand Mausoleums

At the end of nineteenth and in the first decades of the twentieth century, a number of particularly impressive interpretations of Egyptian revival mausoleums reflect the final flowering of Egyptian revival funerary grandeur. Two of these, both located in the same cemetery and designed by the same architect, provide excellent illustrations of this phenomenon. The F.W. Woolworth mausoleum (Fig. 115) in Woodlawn Cemetery, the Bronx, was designed by John Russell Pope using the traditional Egyptian architectural vocabulary found on similar tombs from the nineteenth century but here composed in one of its most elegant and impressive statements.[91] F.W. Woolworth (1853-1919) remains well known across America through the stores that bear his name, and visitors to Woodlawn are enchanted by the striking decorative features which grace his family mausoleum, e.g., the spectacular bronze door featuring three Egyptian figures in low relief who exchange the ankh, the Egyptian symbol of life, and the female sphinxes which flank the front steps. Though exceptionally well conceived, the Woolworth mausoleum certainly did not represent a unique configuration: for example, the Tate Mausoleum in Bellefontaine Cemetery, St. Louis, which dates approximately 1907, shares many of the same design features, with a more masculine pair of bearded sphinxes guarding the front entrance and relief columns decorating the side in the pseudoperipteral tradition.

A neighbor to the Woolworth tomb, the Jules Bache mausoleum in Woodlawn (Fig. 116), was also designed by John Russell Pope.[92] The Bache design, as well as the very similar George Blabon mausoleum in Philadelphia's Laurel Hill Cemetery, were inspired by a small Egyptian temple on the island of Philae in the Nile just above the First Cataract. This temple, or pavilion, was constructed during Imperial Roman times and is often referred to as the Kiosk of Trajan or "Pharaoh's Bed." Francis Frith photographed it in 1857, and an original photograph of the site is included in his *Egypt and Palestine, Photographed and Described* (Fig. 117). When the first dam was constructed at Aswan in 1895-96, this small island was destined to be partially flooded. The controversy over this event which raged in contemporary newspapers helped make the little Philae temple, described as the cradle in which Osiris was reborn, extremely well known outside of Egypt and probably helped encourage its emulation in funerary design.

Cemetery Gates

Because Egyptian architectural forms were traditionally related to the cult of the dead, it is understandable that the style would inspire designers of cemetery portals. This trend was not without its detractors, however: Augustus W.N. Pugin, in his 1843 *An Apology for the Revival of Christian Architecture in England*, illustrated a rather unflattering version of an Egyptianized cemetery entrance, and some Americans seemed to have shared his opinion that the irreverently pagan connotations of the Egyptian style made it inappropriate for Christian use. Certainly the style did not always succeed in pleasing American cemetery associations. When Philadelphia's new rural cemetery, Laurel Hill, was planned in 1836, several proposed entrances inspired by the Egyptian style were submitted for consideration, but John Notman's classical revival design was chosen instead. And Robert Carey Long, Jr. had his Gothic revival portal selected over his Egyptianized gates proposal for Green Mount Cemetery in Baltimore. Nevertheless, a number of distinctive cemetery portals featuring Egyptian motifs were constructed for American cemeteries, one of the earliest examples being the gates (carriage entrance) to Westminster Cemetery in Baltimore (Fig. 118), designed around 1813-15 by Maximilian Godefroy. The stone piers of this extant carriage entrance are topped by Egyptian gorge cornices, with obelisks in relief decorating the front.

Perhaps the best known of the Egyptian style cemetery entrances is that to Mount Auburn Cemetery in Cambridge, Massachusetts (Fig. 119), designed by Dr. Jacob Bigelow and first constructed of wood in 1832, then repro-

Fig. 115. F.W. Woolworth mausoleum, Woodlawn Cemetery, the Bronx, New York. Photo by Harold Allen.

Fig. 116. Jules Bache mausoleum, Woodlawn Cemetery, the Bronx, New York. Photo by Harold Allen.

Fig. 117. The Kiosk of Trajan, or "Pharaoh's Bed," photographed by Francis Frith, from *Egypt and Palestine, Photographed and Described* (1859).

Fig. 118. Carriage entrance to Westminster Cemetery, Baltimore. Photo by Harold Allen.

Fig. 119. Entrance to Mount Auburn Cemetery, Cambridge, Massachusetts. Photo by Fay Foto.

duced in stone ten years later.[93] The entrance
is dominated by a central pylon with flanking
lodges. A massive winged orb with serpent
hovers above the inscription, which reads:

THEN SHALL THE DUST RETURN
TO THE EARTH, AS IT WAS.
AND THE SPIRIT SHALL RETURN
UNTO GOD WHO GAVE IT.

The roll molding that borders the lintel
atop the center gate opening is ornamented by
the popular bound ribbon motif, and the
cavetto cornice is further decorated with vertical layered bands which, like the other design
elements, can be found on several pylons illustrated in the Napoleonic *Description de l'Égypte*,
especially in Volumes Three and Four of this
series (see Fig. 120). Similar details are also
illustrated in Denon's *Voyages dans la Basse et la
Haute Egypte*. It is very likely that Dr. Bigelow
used the *Description* as an inspiration for the
design; however, certain departures are obvious as well. The weightiness of the lintel and
Egyptian gorge cornice of the Mount Auburn
portal, for instance, is proportionately unlike
its potential prototypes. The heavy cast iron
fence that extends from the entrance at Mount
Auburn has stone obelisk posts ornamenting it,
and the cast iron fence posts that connect the
panels feature inverted lotuses decorating the
post base and shafts that are ribbon-wrapped
like the pylon roll molding on the stone gate.

The entrance to the Granary Burying
Ground in Boston (Fig. 121), one of the most
historically important early colonial graveyards
in America, was designed by Isaiah Rogers and
erected in 1841 by Solomon Willard. This
pylon configuration uses the highly traditional
funerary symbol of inverted torches as reliefs
on the posts, with the winged orb on the center top providing the only other decoration.
Through this portal, the visitor can see an
oblique pyramid erected by Willard and dedicated to the parents of Benjamin Franklin
(Franklin himself is buried in Philadelphia).
This form, along with several classical revival
monuments in the rear of the graveyard,
seems strangely out of place amidst the neatly

rearranged rows of early American slate tomb-
stones. A duplicate of the Granary Burying
Ground gate was produced in 1843 by Isaiah
Rogers for the old Touro Jewish Cemetery in
Newport, Rhode Island.

The Grove Street Cemetery entrance in
New Haven, Connecticut (Fig. 122) was
designed by Henry Austin and constructed
1845-1848. Its basic characteristics very much
resemble those of Egyptian revival mausoleum
facades such as previously seen in the
Johnston and Woolworth designs (Figs. 111
and 115). Along with the traditional Egyptian
revival architectural features frequently utilized
in such contexts, this portal employs as well a
variation of the bundled column and bud capital, an element also favored by designers using
Egyptian sources for tomb facades (see, for
instance, the Ball and Johnston mausoleums,
Figs. 110 and 111). The Grove street Cemetery
gate is further enhanced by the effective contrast of textures and shadows that play across
the surfaces and architectural details of the
stone.

In Philadelphia, the Mikveh Israel
Cemetery *metaher*, or receiving house, and
entrance (Fig. 123) was begun in 1847 after
the plan of architect Napoleon LeBrun.
LeBrun had studied in the firm of Thomas U.
Walters, who in 1836 had submitted an
Egyptian portal design for Laurel Hill
Cemetery. No longer extant, the structure was
ornamented by a corbelled central door with
comparable false doors on either side, an effect
which Walters had used in his Laurel Hill proposal. The Mikveh Israel entrance of stuccoed
brick featured slightly battered walls ornamented with wood roll wrapped moldings. The
wooden cornice trimmed in sheet metal
employed the cavetto configuration. At least
two synagogues in Philadelphia were also built
in the Egyptian revival style, which was historically related to the Jewish people and their
years of bondage in that land. The Mikveh
Israel archives include letters from John
Linsay (June 11, 1847) agreeing to build the
entrance house "after the plans of N. Lebrun,"
and from LeBrun himself (April 5, 1847) sub-
mitting his bid for design of the entrance.[94]

Fig. 120. Illustration of portal, from *Description de l'Égypte....*

Fig. 121. Entrance to The Granary Burying Ground, Boston. Photo by Harold Allen.

Fig. 122. Entrance to Grove Street Cemetery, New Haven, Connecticut. Photo by Harold Allen.

Fig. 123. *Metaher* (receiving house) and entrance, Mikveh Israel Cemetery, Philadelphia. Photo by Harold Allen.

Sphinxes

The sphinx regularly appears along with other Egyptian revival architectural and ornamental motifs in the nineteenth century commemorative arts. Often seen guarding the entrance to a tomb, these leonine-bodied fantasy creatures were frequently associated with the qualities of mystery, protection, endurance, and wisdom. In addition to the traditional guardian role in which the form often functions when used in conjunction with architectural forms, the sphinx was also employed as an independent grave or commemorative marker. Like the Great Sphinx at Giza, the most traditional version featured the combination of a lion's body and a man's head. Other sphinxes, not necessarily authentic or Egyptian in origin, combined features in several ways, often using female heads and breasts, as well as wings, in conjunction with the lion's body. One traditional example of the form (Fig. 124) may be seen in the mid-nineteenth century monument erected above the graves of the Lawler family in Cincinnati's Spring Grove Cemetery.

Dr. Jacob Bigelow, an admirer of Egyptian revival forms and designer of the Egyptian gates to Mount Auburn Cemetery in Cambridge, Massachusetts, commissioned the sculpture of a sphinx to serve as a memorial in Mount Auburn to the Union dead of the Civil War. Designed by Martin Milmore and erected in 1870, this somewhat Americanized sphinx (Fig. 125) featured an eagle's head in the center front of the Egyptian headdress and a star hung around the neck of the female head. Columbia had thus been symbolically combined with the lion as funerary guardian. Inscribed on the base, in Latin on one side and in somewhat loosely translated English on the other, are the words:

AMERICA CONSERVATA
AFRICA LIBERATA
POPULO MAGNO ASSURGENTE
HEROUM SANGUINE FUSO
* * * * *
AMERICAN UNION PRESERVED
AFRICAN SLAVERY DESTROYED
BY THE UPRISING OF A GREAT
    PEOPLE
BY THE BLOOD OF FALLEN HEROES

The sphinx must have been closely associated with Milmore, because when Daniel Chester French created a life-sized bronze relief to commemorate Milmore just to the left of the entrance to Boston's Forest Hills Cemetery, he depicted a poppy-bearing angel of death staying Milmore's hand and chisel as the young sculptor carved a sphinx.

Combinations with Other Revival Forms

It was not unusual to see Egyptian decorative and architectural features eclectically combined with those of other revival styles. When Maximilian Godefroy designed the Baltimore Battle Monument (Fig. 126) commemorating the defenders of Fort McHenry during the 1814 engagement with forces of the British navy, he combined classical and Egyptian elements. In doing so, however, he tempered overt Egyptian motifs with classical concepts, and the immediate effect of the monument is more neoclassical than Egyptian. Perhaps it might be argued that this eclectic assimilation made the introduction of the Egyptian stylistic elements more acceptable in some manner to the neophyte American culture. A similar stylistically eclectic assemblage with a mastaba base topped by a classical column is found in the mid-nineteenth century Henry Clay Monument (see Fig. 47) in the Lexington Cemetery, Lexington, Kentucky, the cornerstone of which was laid July 4, 1857 and the work completed in 1861. The Clay Monument Association, consisting of fifteen leading Kentucky statesmen, had to choose from numerous designs submitted from across the United States. Julius W. Adams, a Lexington architect and civil engineer, ultimately submitted the winning design for the monument as a whole, while the fourteen-foot figure of Clay was conceived by Joel T. Hart and carved by Giancorno Bossi and Barabin Giannini. The mausoleum base employs several Egyptian elements: this struc-

Fig. 124. Lawler monument, Spring Grove Cemetery, Cincinnati. Photo by Harold Allen.

Fig. 125. Memorial to The Union Dead of the Civil War, Mount Auburn Cemetery, Cambridge, Massachusetts. Photo by Harold Allen.

Fig. 126. Baltimore Battle Monument, Baltimore. Photo by Lightner Photography.

ture, however, is dominated by a monumental classical column topped by the figure of Clay. Although the height of the column is quite impressive as it elevates the figure heavenward, it also unfortunately renders the pinnacle figure somewhat vulnerable. Like many of the figures placed atop tall shafts, the Clay sculpture was struck by lightning on more than one occasion, and the original figure had to be replaced.[95] As we have seen, both Godefroy and Adams chose in designing these monuments to combine an Egyptian base with a classical superstructure. This could perhaps be interpreted as symbolically representing a chronological ordering—the Egyptian pre-dating the classical cultures. From a purely practical standpoint, however, it is also clear that the sturdy weight of the Egyptian forms serves both functionally and aesthetically to support the lighter classical elements.

The Jonathan Maxcy Monument (Fig. 127) on the University of South Carolina campus in Columbia, erected in 1827 as a memorial to the institution's first president, freely combines classical with Egyptian elements, a style which its designer, Robert Mills, knew well. In the eclectic fashion typical of Mills, the pedestal die combines classical details, anthemion and triangular pediments, atop an Egyptian gorge cornice ornamented on each side with the winged disc (Mills used this same combination in his original design for the entablature of the doors for the Washington Monument in the District of Columbia). The tapering shaft of the Maxcy Monument, which recalls the obelisk, features a band around the middle section with an "M" for Maxcy on the front and stars on the other sides. The tripod on the top again borrows from the classical and refers to the ancient choragic monuments. The square base that elevates the pedestal and shaft is gray granite with marble inscription slabs lettered in Latin, and the superstructure is white marble.

Gothic elements in combination with an Egyptian obelisk may be seen in the Saratoga Battle Monument (Fig. 128), located on the Saratoga Battlefield in Schuyerville, New York, and designed in 1877 by Jared Clark Markham. Here, superimposition of Gothic

architectural motifs onto an obelisk effectively combines the vertical emphasis of the pointed arch with the vertical thrust of the obelisk.

Near Eastern, "Oriental," or Islamic Influences

Romantic literature, the Napoleonic expeditions, and North African colonization furthered an interest in not only contemporary Egypt but also other non-Western cultures influenced by the Islamic religion. Nineteenth-century Egyptians professed an exotic Islamic cultural heritage like that of the Turks of Byron's poems, the Spanish Moors, the Algerians, and the Mughals of India. The Muslim background of Egypt helped further the categorization of medieval through nineteenth century Egyptian art as "Oriental," a term popularly used by nineteenth century architects. Confusion still exists concerning what might constitute an ideal stylistic descriptive term for the art produced in these lands dominated by the teachings of Islam. General and somewhat misleading names such as Moorish, Turkish, Near Eastern, and Mohammedan, as well as Oriental, have been broadly applied to secular and non-secular arts of Islamic peoples stretching from India to Morocco. Christian Byzantine art elements shared by Islamic neighbors have also been commonly grouped into this conglomerate categorization. To name an art style for the main religion of a culture, regardless of the art's intent, its location, or its chronology, would seem somewhat indiscriminative. There was, however, an interaction between Islamic religious and secular arts, especially in the influences which the decorative arts exerted upon concepts of beauty and the ideal spiritual environment. A number of similar design elements associated with the art and architecture of Islamic and Near Eastern cultures, such as the bulbous dome, the horseshoe arch, and intertwining patterned motifs, were commonly employed and served to give the art some sense of identity or continuity. Such features were often considered to be picturesque as well as exotic.

Fig. 127. Jonathan Maxcy monument, University of South Carolina, Columbia, South Carolina. Photo by Harold Allen.

Fig. 128. Saratoga Battle Monument, Schuyerville, New York. Photo Courtesy New York State Department of Commerce.

In America, architects such as Alexander Jackson Davis and Samuel Sloan demonstrated interest in "Oriental" variations in their designs; however, the style was never as popular as other revival modes. Funerary architecture inspired by Islamic designs does not appear in America to any appreciable degree until the late nineteenth century, and when employed it usually is associated with mausoleum designs. In the 1844 *Guide to Laurel Hill* (i.e., Laurel Hill Cemetery, Philadelphia), the author recognizes various cultures that were known for their cemeteries, stating: "The Etruscans, the Greeks, the Romans, and in more modern times the Turks, all illustrated not only their skill in the arts, and their intellectual excellence, but also their social affections and refinement, and all the gentler characteristics of civilization, by a studied attention to cemeteries for the dead." Examples of older extant cemeteries from cultures such as the "Turks" are somewhat sparse, but sufficient to illustrate that a variety of approaches were employed in the funerary arts. Tombs from Islamic cultures are especially impressive and vary from elevated barrel-topped sarcophagi to tower tombs and domed mausoleums. Nineteenth century Western architects did not attempt to precisely duplicate these non-Christian monuments, probably because there were such limited examples in available publications. The grandiose Taj Mahal was occasionally depicted, and in Volume I ("Modern Egypt") of the *Description de l'Égypte* series, monuments from the Cairo Cemetery are illustrated in several plates (e.g., see Fig. 129). No early publication of consequence, however, surveyed the richness of the funerary aspects of Islamic architecture. Instead of copying actual monuments, therefore, American architects borrowed some of the more obvious decorative and architectural motifs from relatively generalized "Oriental" or Islamic traditions.

The facade of the Henry P. Voorhees tomb (Fig. 130) in Laurel Hill Cemetery, Philadelphia, which is dated 1860 above the door, reflects a Byzantine-Eastern taste primarily because of the three pointed horseshoe arches across the front. Twisted spiral moldings frame the three arches and ornament the dentiform topped entablature. Despite its exotic flavoring, the iron cross on the door validates a Christian reference. Somewhat more emphatic in its reference is the Charles A. Larendon tomb (Fig. 131) in Metairie Cemetery, New Orleans, erected in the late nineteenth century. The small portico is dominated by ornately patterned cusped, pointed horseshoe arches and a modified dome. In this instance, the apex cross of the Eastern Church serves to reinforce the monument's stylistic origins.

The C.K. Garrison mausoleum (Fig. 132), located in Brooklyn's Green-Wood Cemetery, was considered so noteworthy at the time that it was illustrated in a carriage tour souvenir booklet of foldout prints published in 1882. This ornate central plan mausoleum features a domical vault with a small dome-covered portico opened by trefoil arches. Atop the portico is a small bulbous domed lantern, somewhat reminiscent of a sultan's turban. The tomb, designed by New York architect Griffith Thomas, was probably built in the 1870s following the death of Cornelius K. Garrison's first wife. A financier, former mayor of San Francisco, and owner of a steamship line, the "Commodore", as he was affectionately known, died May 1, 1885.

Two final examples, both twentieth century and located in Metairie Cemetery, New Orleans, indicate the ongoing appeal of monuments exhibiting Eastern influences. The Arthur Barba, Sr. family mausoleum (Fig. 133) was designed and built in the early twentieth century by the Arthur Weiblen firm: its prototype was probably the mausoleum constructed from Louis Sullivan's design for Ellis and Charlotte Wainwright in 1892 and located in Bellefontaine Cemetery, St. Louis. The ornamentation primarily links the monument to Eastern decorative patternization, and the dome reinforces the Byzantine reference. Between approximately 1890 and 1940, the Weiblen firm built several mausoleums in Metairie Cemetery with Eastern flavoring: the Benton W. Cason mausoleum (see Fig. 134) is one of the later and most ornate examples. Here, the pointed horseshoe arch and linear

VUES ET DÉTAILS DESSINÉS DANS LA VILLE DES TOMBEAUX.

Fig. 129. The Cairo Cemetery, from Vol I, *Description de l'Égypte....*

Fig. 130. Henry Voorhees tomb, Laurel Hill Cemetery, Philadelphia. Photo by Drayton Smith.

Fig. 131. Charles Larendon tomb, Metairie Cemetery, New Orleans. Photo by Richard E. Meyer.

We have seen with what pains the most celebrated nations of which history speaks have adorned their places of sepulture and it is from their funeral monuments that we gather much that is known of their civil progress and of their advancement in taste. Is not the story of Egypt written on its pyramids, and is not the chronology of Arabia pictured on its tombs? Is it not on the funeral relics of Greece and Rome that we behold those elegant images of repose and tender sorrow with which they so happily invested the idea of death? Is it not on the urns and sarcophagi of Etrutia that the lover of the noble art of sculpture still gazes with delight? And is it not amid the catacombs, the crypts, and the calvaries of Italy, that the sculptor and painter of the dark ages chiefly present the most splendid specimens of their chisel and their pencil?.... The tomb has, in fact, been the great chronicler of taste throughout the world. In the East, from the hoary pyramid to the modern Arab's grave; in Europe, from the rude tomb of the Druid to the marble mausoleum of the monarch; in America, from the grove which the Indian chief planted round the sepulchre of his son, to the monument which announces to the lovers of freedom the last resting place of Washington.[96]

decorations are clearly inspired by Moorish design; however, the voluptuous shrouded female figure depicted in relief on the bronze door has a decidedly Greek parentage.

5. THE LEGACY OF THE REVIVAL STYLES

Writing in 1846, a critic of contemporary sepulchral monuments offered the following observations:

It is noteworthy that the author of the foregoing, an American, would by the middle

Fig. 132. C.K. Garrison mausoleum, Green-Wood Cemetery, Brooklyn, New York. Photo by Peggy McDowell.

Fig. 133. Arthur Barba mausoleum, Metairie Cemetery, New Orleans. Photo by Peggy McDowell.

Fig. 134. Benton W. Cason mausoleum, Metairie Cemetery, New Orleans. Photo by Peggy McDowell.

of the nineteenth century see the funerary monuments of this country as securely belonging to a proud and distinguished tradition of artistic endeavor which stretched back to the earliest manifestations of high civilization. Certainly he would have viewed the revival styles as forging a critical link in this chain of taste and dignity binding past and present. These grand structures punctuating the landscape of America's newest and finest cemeteries were a sure indication not only of this country's contemporary "arrival" as a place of cultural and civic achievement, but also of the legacy they would bequeath to future generations of admirers.

Today, the visitor to one of America's numerous "rural" cemeteries founded in the middle years of the previous century is sure to encounter this legacy at first hand. What do these monuments, so richly evocative of the glories of past civilizations, tell us of our own civilization and of the people who erected them? At the very least, we see here a clear record and vivid demonstration of our predecessors' strong awareness of history and tradition, not to speak of their value and respect for the individual and for meaningful memorialization. But there is more implied here, certainly. Strolling amongst these beautiful and impressive structures, we by slow degrees might well come to arrive at the same level of understanding as that articulated by Mr. Smith in his comments of a century and a half ago—the notion that, somehow, these monuments created by American hands upon American soil link us inextricably to the very best and most enduring of those great civilizations that preceded us. The revival styles by their very definition sought to reinterpret architectural formulas that were established and reinforced by respected aesthetics, theories, and philosophies. The revival architectural philosophy thus offered reassurance because time had tested and sanctioned its use. What had lasted until now would surely last well into the future, and, like Keats' fabled Grecian urn, would continue to speak to us of the eternal verities of truth and beauty.

From the early nineteenth through the early twentieth centuries, the monument industries thrived in America, producing what arguably might be termed the "golden age" in American funerary art. As the twentieth century matured, new generations with different needs, attitudes, and priorities would focus their attentions elsewhere: philosophical pragmatism, further tempered by the harsh realities of two world wars, and a severe economic depression, effectively turned America's preoccupation with grandiose commemoration into more practical channels. The "rural" cemetery gave way to the "memorial park," and the sculpted or architectural monument to the flattened, artistically nondescript marker. To the observer at mid-century, it must surely have seemed that the American way of death, in our times at least, had ultimately led us to a bland, featureless, and totally uninteresting funerary landscape stretching before us with no immediate prospect for change or revitalization.

This, however, has fortunately not proven to be the case. Recent decades have seen a strong resurgence of interest in meaningful artistic commemoration, and the observable effects within the cemetery are both vivid and dramatic. Chief amongst these are the return of the upright monument and the tremendous increase in the degree of personalized visual and verbal imagery applied to the surface of memorials, the latter enhanced greatly by both patron demand and the application of certain new technologies available to the monument industries. But there is more at work as well. To the close observer, it becomes evident that a number of design traditions established in the nineteenth century still possess great appeal to both the creators and the patrons of contemporary monuments. Leading the way is what might, for lack of a more creative descriptive nomenclature, be termed a revival of the revival styles. This renewed emphasis upon the revival styles is evident not only in the cemetery landscape itself, but in the advertisements and stories found within the pages of contemporary trade publications serving professional memorialists and cemeterians, where, tellingly enough, they once again emphasize strongly the elements of grace, dignity, and timelessness associated with these design styles so loved by our nineteenth century predecessors. Even the revival-inspired private family mausoleum, once seemingly the sole prerogative of the rich and famous in American society, has been reappearing with increasing frequency as a memorial choice amongst patrons of less grand means (see Fig. 135).[97]

And so the legacy of the revival styles is really twofold in nature. Throughout this study we have examined a series of impressive monuments inspired by the architectural heritage of ancient Greece and Rome, the European middle ages, and distant Egypt and the Near East. In the finest tradition of the cemetery as outdoor museum, these monuments—or the vast majority of them at any rate—remain on site, visible reminders of a time when Americans consciously sought in their public and private memorials to recreate

the very best and most beautiful of which civilization had proven capable. Not only that, having leapfrogged a period in the history of American material commemoration in which concerns of beauty and tradition were seemingly overshadowed by more practical considerations, these styles are once again exerting a powerful and exciting influence upon the design of contemporary monuments. It is, indeed, precisely this rich blending of past and present which has made the study of American memorial art, in all of its various manifestations, so fascinating in recent years to scholars and others. As for the future, whatever direction that art may take, whatever influences may ultimately come to bear upon it, it is reasonable to assume that the revival styles will continue to invigorate the imaginations of those desiring to erect meaningful and lasting monuments in memory of those we have loved and cherished.

Fig. 135. Contemporary revival-inspired family mausoleum, designed by Rock of Ages, Barre, Vermont. Woodlawn Cemetery, Everett, Massachusetts. Photo courtesy *Stone in America*.

NOTES

[1]Richard Dana, "The Husband and Wife's Grave," *Harper's New Monthly Magazine* (Dec. 1857), p. 12. *Harper's* frequently published poems that expressed similar sentiments about commemoration.

[2]A rich selection of scholarly works treating the tradition of western funerary arts is available to the interested reader. These range from the broadest possible treatment to more limited, culture-specific assessments. Amongst the many studies which deal primarily with European models (a comprehensive overview of the American experience remains as yet unwritten), the following are particularly recommended: Erwin Panofsky, *Tomb Sculpture: Four Lectures on its Changing Aspects from Ancient Egypt to Bernini*, ed. H.W. Janson (New York, 1964); Howard Colvin, *Architecture and the After-Life* (New Haven, CT, 1991); James Stevens Curl, *A Celebration of Death: An Introduction to Some of the Buildings, Monuments and Settings of Funerary Architecture in the Western European Tradition* (New York, 1980); Michel Ragon, *The Space of Death: A Study of Funerary Architecture, Decoration and Urbanism*, trans. Alan Sheridan (Charlottesville, VA, 1983); Richard A. Etlin, *The Architecture of Death: The Transformation of the Cemetery in Eighteenth-Century Paris* (Cambridge, MA, 1984); Nicholas Penny, *Church Monuments in Romantic England* (New Haven, CT, 1977).

[3]Robert Mills, "Essay on Architectural Monuments," *Analectic Magazine* (April 1820), pp. 277-278.

[4]The quotation is from *Harper's New Monthly Magazine* (March 1859), pp. 433-438.

[5]The roles of Strickland and Struthers in designing and carving the Washington sarcophagi are reported in the *Harper's* article and in Agnes Addison Gilchrist, *William Strickland, Architect and Engineer, 1788-1854*, enlarged ed. (New York, 1969). Gilchrist indicates that the sarcophagi were carved and presented by Struthers at his own expense to Colonel Lawrence Lewis, who had inherited the Mount Vernon estate. In the appendix to her work, the author includes a reference from *The Philadelphia Inquirer* (Sept. 18, 1837) which gives the name of John Hill as the workman who actually carved the sarcophagi. Struthers and Strickland worked together on a large number of buildings and monuments, many of which are included in the enlarged edition of Gilchrist's study. Other data on the history of Washington's tomb may be found in Strickland's *The Tomb of Washington at Mount Vernon* (Philadelphia, 1840).

[6]This original objective of the association is reported in *Mount Vernon: An Illustrated Handbook* (Mount Vernon Ladies' Association of the Union, 1974), p. 8.

[7]Lines 244-251 of the poem as printed in the Sept. 1865 issue of *Atlantic Monthly*. Lowell read his "Commemoration Ode" to Harvard associates before it was subsequently printed in several contemporary publications. Today, the poem is often included in anthologies of American poetry.

[8]Military monuments and war memorials represent a form of funerary art and public commemoration with highly specialized contexts. For an interesting and comprehensive study which surveys the symbolic functions of such artifacts from the American Revolution through the Vietnam conflict, see James M. Mayo, *War Memorials as Political Landscape: The American Experience and Beyond* (New York, 1988). A more restricted but no less revealing analysis is presented in Stephen Davis, "Empty Eyes, Marble Hands: The Confederate Monument and the South," *Journal of Popular Culture* 16:3 (1982), pp. 2-21.

[9]This often quoted address was delivered to thousands of listeners on November 19, 1863.

[10]For example, *The American Architect and Building News* and *The American Art Review*.

[11]Untitled, *The Granite-Cutters Journal* (March 1887), p. 1. This trade journal often printed materials borrowed from other publications.

[12]"The Silent City at Greenwood," *Harper's New Monthly Magazine* (Jan. 1869), p. 160. Green-Wood, a celebrated "rural" cemetery in Brooklyn, New York, is also commonly spelled Greenwood.

[13]"The Living and the Dead," *Frank Leslie's Illustrated Newspaper* (Feb. 25, 1865), p. 362. Happily, not all attempts to write pensive verse about the grave, death, and cemeteries yielded such mawkish results as seen in these three examples. Some of America's more illustrious nineteenth century poets, such as Henry Wadsworth Longfellow and Edgar Allan Poe, contributed worthwhile efforts to the tradition.

[14]A useful overall treatment of the popular and sentimentalized treatments of death and mourning in nineteenth century America is presented in Martha V. Pike and Janice Gray Armstrong, *A Time*

to Mourn: Expressions of Grief in Nineteenth Century America (Stony Brook, NY, 1980).

[15]Many such commemorative lithographs were printed by Currier and Ives and sold in large numbers to be individually personalized by the purchaser. On the general topic of nineteenth century mourning pictures, see Pike and Armstrong, A Time to Mourn. See also Anita Schorsch, "A Key to the Kingdom: The Inconography of a Mourning Picture," Winterthur Portfolio: A Journal of American Material Culture 14:1 (1979), pp. 41-71. For a fascinating review of the popularity of funerary photography, see Stanley B. Burns, Sleeping Beauty: Memorial Photography in America (Altadena, CA, 1990).

[16]A number of these artifacts are discussed and illustrated in Pike and Armstrong, A Time to Mourn.

[17]Late in the nineteenth century Samuel Clemens used the theory that miasmas from cemeteries were responsible for illnesses to encourage Americans to practice cremation. Clemens included some of these ideas in his 1883 Life on the Mississippi; however, his opinions, somewhat controversial and shocking for those times, were deleted from the original edition. An addendum to a 1944 printing of Life on the Mississippi by Heritage Press entitled "The Suppressed Passages" reveals Clemens's opinion that: "You can burn a person for four or five dollars, and you can get soap enough out of his ashes to foot the bill." Clemens, long before the social exposès of Jessica Mitford (The American Way of Death) and others, clearly disliked the American preoccupation with funeral rituals and the expenses associated with death.

[18]Recent studies of the history of Parisian burial practices in the eighteenth century provide valuable information about the influences that led to the establishment of cemeteries such as Père Lachaise. See Etlin, The Architecture of Death, and Frederick Brown, Père Lachaise: Elysium as Real Estate (New York, 1973).

[19]For an examination of these contemporary uses of the cemetery as greenspace in an American context, see Blanche Linden-Ward, "Strange but Genteel Pleasure Grounds: Tourist and Leisure Uses of Nineteenth Century Rural Cemeteries," in Cemeteries and Gravemarkers: Voices of American Culture, ed. Richard E. Meyer (Ann Arbor, MI, 1989; rpt. Logan, UT, 1992), pp. 293-328.

[20]Prospectus of the General Cemetery Company (London, 1830), pp. 30-31.

[21]A comprehensive study of victorian cemeteries is provided in James Stevens Curl, The Victorian Celebration of Death (Detroit, 1972). For specific information on the great metropolitan cemeteries of London founded during this period see Hugh Meller, London Cemeteries: An Illustrated Guide and Gazetteer, 2nd ed. (London, 1985).

[22]Three studies in particular are most illustrative in charting the history and impact of these cemeteries in America. For an exhaustive examination of Mount Auburn, the first of the true rural cemeteries in the United States, see Blanche Linden-Ward, Silent City on a Hill: Landscapes of Memory and Boston's Mount Auburn Cemetery (Columbus, OH, 1989). For more general descriptive and socio-historical overviews see David Charles Sloane, The Last Great Necessity: Cemeteries in American History (Baltimore, 1991), and James J. Farrell, Inventing the American Way of Death, 1830-1920 (Philadelphia, 1980), especially Chapter 4, "The Development of the Modern Cemetery," pp. 99-145. In point of fact, regional cemeteries had been established at an earlier point in New Orleans, a city famous for its "Cities of the Dead." The unique environment in lower Louisiana encouraged early settlers to establish regional cemeteries for use by the religious community. These early graveyards were placed on the fringes of neighborhoods, and as the city expanded more cemeteries were established. Among the first were St. Louis Cemetery I, opened in 1789, followed by St. Louis Cemetery II in 1823. See Leonard V. Huber, Peggy McDowell, and Mary Louise Christovich, New Orleans Architecture: Vol. III, The Cemeteries (Gretna, LA, 1974).

[23]See Linden-Ward, "Strange but Genteel Pleasure Grounds...."

[24]Which should not be taken to imply that stonecarving talent was absent prior to this time. Indeed, the folk carving tradition as applied to American gravemarkers was an extraordinarily rich one dating from the latter years of the sixteenth century, and its history has been well documented in the literature. The point here is that, despite the richness of individual talent prior to the nineteenth century, or even the establishment during this formative period of several "shops" centered about certain particularly talented and entrepreneurial carvers, the production of monuments in America had yet to reach the stage where it might legitimately be termed an industry and its craftsmen professionals.

[25]Much valuable information on the industry, its union activities, and the monuments it produced may be found in a trade publication entitled The Granite-Cutters Journal, which was published in the latter decades of the nineteenth century. The history of one quarry nexus—perhaps the most renowned of them all—is provided in Rod Clarke, Carved in Stone: A History of the Barre Granite Industry (Barre, VT, 1989).

[26]Wayne Andrews, Architecture, Ambition and Americans: A Social History of American Architecture (New York, 1964), p. 104.

[27]Harper's New Monthly Magazine 44 (1871), p. 28.

[28]Studies of the tombstone-type gravemarkers of this period, as well as the known folk carvers who produced them, are numerous and account for a major portion of the significant scholarship on American funerary art produced to date. Amongst book-length treatments, the following are particularly recommended: Peter Benes, *The Masks of Orthodoxy: Folk Gravestone Carving in Plymouth County, Massachusetts, 1689-1805* (Amherst, MA, 1977); Theodore Chase and Laurel Gabel, *Gravestone Chronicles: Some Eighteenth-Century New England Carvers and Their Work* (Boston, 1990); Diana Williams Combs, *Early Gravestone Art in Georgia and South Carolina* (Athens, GA, 1986); Harriette Merrifield Forbes, *Gravestones of Early New England and the Men Who Made Them, 1653-1800* (Boston, 1927; rpt. Brooklyn, NY, 1989); Allan I. Ludwig, *Graven Images: New England Stonecarving and Its Symbols, 1650-1815* (Middletown, CT, 1966); James A. Slater, *The Colonial Burying Grounds of Eastern Connecticut and the Men Who Made Them* (Hamden, CT, 1987); Dickran and Ann Tashjian, *Memorials for Children of Change: The Art of Early New England Stonecarving* (Middletown, CT, 1974); Deborah Trask, *Life How Short, Eternity How Long: Gravestone Carving and Carvers in Nova Scotia* (Halifax, 1978); David H. Watters, *'With Bodilie Eyes': Eschatological Themes in Puritan Literature and Gravestone Art* (Ann Arbor, MI, 1981); Richard F. Welch, *Mememto Mori: The Gravestones of Early Long Island, 1680-1810* (Syosset, NY, 1983). Excellent studies of individual stonecarvers may be found in the two volumes produced by the Dublin Seminar for New England Folklife, *Puritan Gravestone Art* (Boston, 1977; rpt., Worcester, MA, 1993) and *Puritan Gravestone Art II* (Boston, 1978; rpt., Worcester, MA, 1993), and in the many annual volumes of *Markers: Journal of the Association for Gravestone Studies* published from 1980 until the present. For a brief but illuminating overview of the functional and symbolic role of the graveyard in early American life, see John R. Stilgoe, *Common Landscape of America, 1580 to 1845* (New Haven, CT, 1982), pp. 219-231.

[29]See *Bruton Parish Churchyard and Church: A Guide to the Tombstones, Monuments and Mural Tablets* (Williamsburg, VA, 1976).

[30]A limited but quite striking selection of color photographs illustrating these forms, as well as those associated with the medieval and Egyptian revivals, may be found in the relevant sections of Kenneth T. Jackson and Camilo José Vergara, *Silent Cities: The Evolution of the American Cemetery* (New York, 1989).

[31]A few commemorative arches in the tradition of the Roman triumphal arch were constructed. Examples include the Dewey Arch (1899), the Washington Arch by Stanford White (1895), and the Victory Arch by Thomas Hastings (1919).

[32]For an in-depth study of de Pouilly's achievements, see Peggy McDowell, "J. N. B. de Pouilly and French Sources of Revival Style Design in New Orleans Cemetery Architecture," in *Cemeteries and Gravemarkers: Voices of American Culture*, ed. Richard E. Meyer (Ann Arbor, MI, 1989; rpt. Logan, UT, 1992), pp. 137-158.

[33]John Haviland, *Practical Builder's Assistant* (Baltimore, 1830), p. 78.

[34]p. 10. The article gives very little information about H. Q. French, but does note that "His productions are seen all over the country. Among those recently built are Mr. Jay Gould's and Mr. Henry Hurlbut's at Woodlawn; Mr. Robert L. Stuart's and Mr. Peter Gilsey's at Greenwood; Mr, John C. Crouse's at Syracuse, N.Y.; the "Bodmann," at Cincinnati, Ohio; the "Ransom" (sic), at Macon, Ga., and a long list of less expensive ones in various places." The Ransone tomb in Rose Hill Cemetery, Macon, Georgia, is dated on the inscription slab as 1880. It is constructed of weighty rusticated granite courses of stone without reference to any revival style. The Richards mausoleum in Oakland Cemetery, Atlanta, a tomb signed by French, is discussed and illustrated in the Gothic revival section of this study.

[35]Data on this firm and its works may be found in Leland M. Roth, *The Architecture of McKim, Mead, and White, 1870-1920: A Building List* (New York, 1978). The large collection of drawings, blueprints, and other data in the McKim, Mead, and White Archives of the New York Historical Society also provides useful information about commemorative monuments designed by this firm, which employed a large number of architects, builders, and draftsmen. The presence of this material is invaluable, all the more so since data on tombs of this period was often discarded and the names of the designers and firms responsible not preserved.

[36]Prices are given in Roth's *The Architecture of McKim, Mead, and White*: he collected the data from the firm's account books.

[37]Allegorical figures, often four in number when a square base was used, are a feature one also frequently encounters on commemorative military monuments dating from the latter part of the nineteenth century.

[38]*The New York Times Supplement* for Sunday, April 25, 1897 featured the history and description of the monument. Various articles in this newspaper reported the proceedings and controversies of the Association during the decade before the tomb was built.

[39]As reported in *The New York Times*, Sept. 12, 1890, p. 8.

[40]See *The New York Times*, Sept. 10, 1890, p. 8, and Sept. 13, 1890, p. 4.

[41]Information on this and other presidents' tombs can be found in Archibald Laird, *Monuments Marking the Graves of the Presidents* (Hanover, MA, 1971) and Joseph O'Donnell, *The Paths of Glory: A Guide to the Gravesites of Our Deceased Presidents* (West Bethesda, MD, 1992).

[42]*Gettysburg, The National Shrine*, rev. ed. (Gettysburg, PA, 1975), p. 27.

[43]The illustration is taken from *Harper's New Monthly Magazine*, Vol. 51, No. 302, p. 177.

[44]Further analysis of this monument may be found in Daniel D. Reiff, "The Whitefield Cenotaph: A Rediscovered Work by William Strickland," *Journal of the Society for Architectural Historians* 33:1 (1974): pp. 48-60.

[45]Benjamin H. B. Latrobe, *Impressions Respecting New Orleans*, ed. Samuel Wilson, Jr. (New York, 1951), p. 99. Reproduced on the same page is a Latrobe sketch of a square monument with a foundation designed to stabilize the weight.

[46]"Early Settler Memorials—IX," *The American Architect and Building News* (May 7, 1887): p. 219.

[47]Interestingly enough, there is still some controversy as to whether in fact Boone is buried beneath the Kentucky monument which bears his name or remains in Missouri. This matter was treated at some length in a paper by Maryellen McVicker, "Is Daniel Boone Buried in Kentucky?", delivered at the 1992 American Culture Association annual meeting in Louisville, Kentucky.

[48]Latrobe, *Impressions Respecting New Orleans*, p. 100.

[49]Data furnished by Arlington National Cemetery.

[50]Data furnished by Arlington National Cemetery. Additional information may be found in James Edward Peters, *Arlington National Cemetery: Shrine to America's Heroes* (Kensington, MD, 1986), pp. 278-286.

[51]T.H. Bartlett, "Civic Monuments in New England," *The American Architect and Building News* (June, 1881), p. 303.

[52]Data on the Douglas monument can be found in the *Chicago Tribune*, North Neighborhood News, July 8, 1865, pp. 1 and 3. The design was reproduced and described several times in *Harper's Weekly* (see issues of Oct, 1, 1864 and Sept. 15 1866). *Harper's New Monthly Magazine*, in its October, 1880 issue, illustrates the final phase of the completed monument without the base sculptures.

[53]An evaluation of Mill's designs and a discussion of possible prototypes, including Sir Christopher Wren's design for a column commemorating those who died in the Great Fire of London, is discussed in J. Jefferson Miller II, "The Designs for the Washington Monument in Baltimore," *Journal of the Society of Architectural Historians* 23 (March 1964): pp. 18-28.

[54]The poem is by H. F. Requier, Esq., and was published in *Ceremonies Connected with the Unveiling of the Statue of General Robert E. Lee at Lee Circle, New Orleans, La., Feb. 22, 1884* (New Orleans, 1884). A copy of this booklet, which reprints the ceremony along with a historical sketch of the Lee Monumental Association, is in the possession of the Historic New Orleans Collection.

[55]James Jackson Jarvis, *Art Thoughts* (Cambridge, MA, 1869), p. 302.

[56]*Ibid.*

[57]For further analysis of the column as civic monument and the Boston Common Civil War Monument, see Peggy McDowell, "Martin Milmore's Soldiers and Sailors Monument on the Boston Common: Formulating Conventionalism in Design and Symbolism," *Journal of American Culture* 11:1 (Spring 1988): pp. 63-86.

[58]John Francis Stanley, "The Exedra in Memorial Design," in *Memorial Art, Ancient and Modern*, ed. Harry Bliss (Buffalo, NY, 1912), p. 98. Bliss' work as a whole is an excellent source for an understanding of revival designs built at the turn of the century. Stanley is identified in the book as a New York monument designer.

[59]*Ibid.*, p. 101.

[60]Saint-Gaudens' famous sculpture is sometimes referred to in guidebooks and other sources by the title *Grief*. An interesting recent interpretation of the monument was provided by Charles Vandersee in "Grave Site as Gift and Prophecy: The Adams Monument at Rock Creek Cemetery," a paper delivered at the 1993 American Culture Association annual meeting in New Orleans, Louisiana.

[61]"The Farragut Monument," *Scribner's Monthly* 22:2 (June 1881): p. 166.

[62]Information concerning the Missouri and Iowa Monuments supplied by Vicksburg National Military Park.

[63]Chester Hills, *The Builder's Guide*, Vol. II (Hartford, CT, 1834), p. 25.

[64]Charles L. Eastlake, *A History of the Gothic Revival* (London, 1872), p. 176.

[65]In *The Works of Ruskin*, Vol. IX, ed. E.T. Cook and Alexander Wedderburn (London, 1903), p. 177. The monument is illustrated from Ruskin's drawing, plate D. Richard Parks Bennington also illustrated the Castelbarco tomb in a watercolor dated 1827, now in the collection of the Nottingham Castle Museum.

[66]Lines 343-344; 352. In *Eighteenth Century Poetry and Prose*, ed. Louis I. Bredvold, Alan D. McKillop, and Lois Whitney. 2nd Ed. (New York, 1956), pp. 369-370.

[67]John Ruskin, *The Lamp of Beauty*, ed. Joan Evans (London, 1959), p. 240.

[68]"Monuments," *The American Architect and Building News* (August 6, 1887): p. 59.

[69]The image of the broken rose stem, emblematic of a life cut short in the height of its bloom, was one of the most pervasive verbal (and visual) motifs in nineteenth century funerary art pertaining to the deaths of children and young adults. See Deborah A. Smith, "'Safe in the Arms of Jesus': Consolation on Delaware Children's Gravestones, 1840-99," *Markers: Journal of the Association for Gravestone Studies* 4 (1987): pp. 85-106.

[70]John Jay Smith, *Designs for Monuments and Mural Tablets Adapted to Rural Cemeteries and Church Yards* (Philadelphia, 1846), p. 40.

[71]*A Concise Glossary of Architecture* (Oxford, 1888).

[72]Nehemiah Cleveland, *Green-Wood: A Directory for Visitors* (New York, 1857). p. 147.

[73]Information furnished by Hollywood Cemetery. For additional information, see Mary H. Mitchell, *Hollywood Cemetery: The History of a Southern Shrine* (Richmond, VA, 1985).

[74]On a far less grand scale, one may note the prominence of Gothic design elements in the many lych gates which formed the entrances to countless European (and even, upon occasion, American) churchyards: see D. Gregory Jeane, "The Upland South Folk Cemetery Complex: Some Suggestions of Origin," in *Cemeteries and Gravemarkers: Voices of American Culture*, ed. Richard E. Meyer (Ann Arbor, MI, 1989; rpt. Logan, UT, 1992), pp. 126; 130-132. Harriette M. Forbes, better known for her pioneering studies of American colonial gravestones and their carvers, even noted such features in the cast iron gates found in many New England cemeteries: see her "Symbolic Cemetery Gates in New England," and Margot Gayle's companion piece, "A Portfolio of Harriette Forbes's Cast-Iron Gates," both found in *Markers: Journal of the Association for Gravestone Studies* 7 (1990): pp. 3-18; 19-33.

[75]Laurence Bradford, *Historic Duxbury in Plymouth County* (Boston, 1900), pp. 39-41.

[76]"'The Good Old Times' at Plymouth," *Harper's New Monthly Magazine* 54 (Dec. 1876-May 1877): p. 180.

[77]See T.H. Bartlett, "Early Settler Memorials," *The American Architect and Building News* (Nov. 6, 1886): pp. 216-217.

[78]The painting is discussed on pp. 212-213 and illustrated in plate 20 of Louis Legrand Noble's *The Life and Works of Thomas Cole*, ed. Elliott S. Vesell (Cambridge, MA, 1964).

[79]There were subsequent editions of this massive work reprinted in varying combinations of volumes.

[80]Haviland, *Practical Builder's Assistant*, p. 89.

[81]T.H. Bartlett, "Early Settler Memorials," *The American Architect and Building News* (Dec. 4, 1886), p. 56. The T.H. Bartlett who wrote this interesting series of articles in 1886-87 for *The American Architect and Building News* was Truman Howe Bartlett (1835-1923), a New England sculptor who had studied and traveled in Europe and who taught at the Massachusetts Institute of Technology. He wrote extensively for this journal, and his criticism, though often strongly worded, frequently reveals the insight of a sensitive artist and educator.

[82]Henry Van Brunt, "The Washington Monument," *The American Art Review* 1 (1880): p. 9.

[83]Quoted in *The American Architect and Building News* (April 28, 1888): p. 200. For other pertinent data on Jefferson, see Fiske Kimball, *Thomas Jefferson, Architect and Builder* (Cambridge, MA, 1916).

[84]Information on the Confederate Monument was furnished by Hollywood Cemetery. For additional detail, see Mitchell, *Hollywood Cemetery: The History of a Southern Shrine*.

[85]Smith, *Designs for Monuments and Mural Tablets Adapted to Rural Cemeteries and Church Yards*, p. 29.

[86](London, 1859-1860).

[87]The fascination with things Egyptian—and with King Tutankhamen in particular—has never really disappeared in America, as most recently witnessed by the highly successful "Treasures of Tutankhamen" traveling exhibition which appeared in major museums across the nation in the mid-1970s.

[88](June 10, 1847): p. 2. Information on this and a number of other Egyptian monuments was found in the extensive collection of Harold Allen, a pioneering scholar and photographer of the Egyptian Revival, to whom the authors express their grateful debt.

[89]The original drawings for this tomb are in the archives of the Historical Society of Pennsylvania in Philadelphia.

[90]For a thoroughgoing analysis of Louis Sullivan and the Ryerson mausoleum, as well as his two other famous mausoleum designs, the Getty tomb in Graceland Cemetery, and the Wainwright tomb in St. Louis' Bellefontaine Cemetery, see Robert A. Wright, "Poems in Stone: The Tombs of Louis Henri Sullivan," *Markers: Journal of the Association for Gravestone Studies* 5 (1988): pp. 168-208. Other, sometimes more exotic parallels of the Ryerson mausoleum have also been noted, including the remarkably similar "Turkish tent" design by Carol Frederik Adelcranz constructed in Drottningholm, Sweden in 1781.

[91]Pope was obviously comfortable with more than one of the revival styles, as evidenced by his later design for the classically inspired Jefferson Memorial (dedicated 1943) in Washington, D.C.

[92]The Woolworth and Bache mausoleums, as well as a number of other elaborate revival style tombs in Woodlawn Cemetery, are described briefly

and beautifully illustrated in Edward F. Bergman, *Woodlawn Remembers: Cemetery of American History* (Utica, NY, 1988).

[93]See Richard G. Carrott, *The Egyptian Revival: Its Sources, Monuments and Meaning, 1808-1859* (Berkeley, CA, 1978), p. 87. A number of other illustrations of Egyptian revival cemetery gates are also included within this study. On Dr. Jacob Bigelow and his architectural and other contributions to Mount Auburn Cemetery, see Linden-Ward, *Silent City on a Hill: Landscapes of Memory and Boston's Mount Auburn Cemetery.* A number of other seminal treatments of this subject are available, including Barbara Rotundo, "Mount Auburn Cemetery: A Proper Boston Institution," *Harvard Library Bulletin* 22:3 (1974): pp. 268-279; and Stanley French, "The Cemetery as Cultural Institution: The Establishment of Mount Auburn and the 'Rural Cemetery' Movement," *American Quarterly* 26 (1974): pp. 37-59.

[94]Data on the Mikveh Israel Cemetery *metaher* and entrance was provided by the private collection and archives of Harold Allen.

[95]Information on the Clay Monument was furnished by the Fayette County, Kentucky, Library. See also Coleman J. Winston, Jr., *Historic Kentucky* (Lexington, KY, 1967).

[96]Smith, *Designs for Monuments and Mural Tablets Adapted to Rural Cemeteries and Church Yards*, p. 7.

[97]The *scale* of these newer mausoleums is, of course, greatly reduced, as is the size of the cemetery real estate on which they tend to be situated. This, plus newer and more efficient concepts in fabrication and construction, has been instrumental in making such options accessible to families with names less instantaneously recognizable than Woolworth, Armour, or Steinway. On the resurgence of the mausoleum, as described in a major trade journal serving the monument industry, see Susan Opt Whitlock, "Mausoleums," *Stone in America* (December, 1986): pp. 18-25; Jacqueline Hanks, "Mausoleum Design," *Stone in America* (November, 1990): pp. 12-19; and Lee Jansen, "Affordable Affluence," *Stone in America* (May, 1993): pp. 30-34.

BIBLIOGRAPHY

Addison, Agnes. *Romanticism and the Gothic Revival.* New York, 1967.

Alexander, Robert L. "The Public Memorial and Godefroy's Battle Monument." *Journal of the Society of Architectural Historians* 17 (1958): 19-24.

Allen, Harold. "My Egypt." *Exposure* 16.1 (1978): 16-27.

Alverson, Fred. "Spring Grove Cemetery." *Stone in America* (Sept. 1986): 32-49.

Ambler, Cathy. "A Place Not Entirely of Sadness and Gloom: Oak Hill and the Rural Cemetery Movement." *Kansas History* 15.4 (1992-93): 240-253.

Ames, Kenneth L. *Death in the Dining Room and Other Tales of Victorian Culture.* Philadelphia, 1992.

_____. "Ideologies in Stone: Meanings in Victorian Gravestones." *Journal of Popular Culture* 14.4 (1981): 641-656.

Andrews, Wayne. *Architecture, Ambition and Americans: A Social History of American Architecture.* New York, 1964.

Arbeiter, Jean and Linda D. Cirino. *Permanent Addresses: A Guide to the Resting Places of Famous Americans.* New York, 1983.

Ariès, Philippe. *The Hour of Our Death.* Trans. Helen Weaver. New York, 1981.

_____. *Images of Man and Death.* Trans. Janet Lloyd. Cambridge, MA, 1985.

_____. "The Reversal of Death: Changes in Attitudes Toward Death in Western Societies." *American Quarterly* 26.5 (1974): 536-560.

_____. *Western Attitudes Toward Death From the Middle Ages to the Present.* Trans. Patricia N. Ranum. Baltimore, 1974.

Arnot, David Henry. *Gothic Architecture Applied to Modern Residences.* New York, 1849.

Bandiera, John D. "The City of the Dead: French Eighteenth-Century Designs for Funerary Complexes." *Gazette des Beaux Arts* 101 (1983): 25-33.

Barber, Bernard. "Place, Symbol and Utilitarian Function in War Memorials." *Social Forces* 28 (1949): 64-68.

Barker, Felix and John Gayn. *Highgate Cemetery: Victorian Valhalla.* Salem, NH, 1984.

Barth, Gunther. *Fleeting Moments: Nature and Culture in American History.* New York, 1990.

Bartlett, T.H. "Early Settler Memorials." *The American Architect and Building News.* (Series of articles on American monuments published 1886-1887).

Bender, Thomas. "The Rural Cemetery Movement: Urban Travail and the Appeal of Nature." *The New England Quarterly* 47 (1974): 196-211.

_____. *Towards an Urban Vision.* Lexington, KY, 1975.

Benes, Peter. *The Masks of Orthodoxy: Folk Gravestone Carving in Plymouth County, Massachusetts, 1689-1805.* Amherst, MA, 1977.

Benjamin, Asher. *The American Builder's Companion.* Boston, 1827.

_____. *The Builder's Guide.* Boston, 1839.

Bergman, Edward F. *Woodlawn Remembers: Cemetery of American History.* Utica, NY, 1988.

Bigelow, Jacob. *A History of the Cemetery of Mount Auburn.* Boston, 1860.

Bliss, Harry A., ed. *Memorial Art, Ancient and Modern.* Buffalo, 1912.

Boatner, Mark M., III. *Landmarks of the American Revolution.* Harrisburg, PA, 1973.

Bohan, Ruth L. "A Home Away From Home: Bellefontaine Cemetery, St. Louis, and the Rural Cemetery Movement." *Prospects: An Annual of American Cultural Studies* 13 (1988): 135-79.

Bradford, Laurence. *Historic Duxbury in Plymouth County.* Boston, 1900.

Brangwyn, W.C. *Gothic Memorials.* Wolverhampton, England, 1861.

Brooks, Chris. *Mortal Remains: The History and Present State of the Victorian and Edwardian Cemetery.* Exeter, England, 1989.

Brown, Frederick. *Pére Lachaise: Elysium as Real Estate*. New York, 1979.

Bruton Parish Churchyard and Church: A Guide to the Tombstones, Monuments and Mural Tablets. Williamsburg, VA, 1976.

Bryan, John A. *A Journey Through History: Touring Bellefontaine Cemetery*. St. Louis, 1983.

Burchard, John, and Albert Bush-Brown. *The Architecture of America: A Social and Cultural History*. Boston, 1961.

Burgess, Frederick. *English Churchyard Memorials*. London, 1963.

Burgess, Pamela. *Churchyards*. London, 1980.

Burns, Stanley B. *Sleeping Beauty: Memorial Photography in America*. Altadena, CA, 1990.

Butler, John V. *Churchyards of Trinity Parish in the City of New York, 1697-1969*. New York, 1969.

Butler, Ruth. *Western Sculpture: Definitions of Man*. New York, 1975.

Carrott, Richard G. *The Egyptian Revival: Its Sources, Monuments, and Meaning, 1808-1858*. Berkeley, 1978.

Ceremonies Connected With the Unveiling of the Statue of General Robert E. Lee at Lee Circle, New Orleans, La., Feb. 22, 1884. New Orleans, 1884.

Chase, David B. "The Beginnings of the Landscape Tradition in America." *Historic Preservation* 25 (1973): 41.

Chase, Theodore and Laurel Gabel. *Gravestone Chronicles: Some Eighteenth-Century New England Carvers and Their Work*. Boston, 1990.

Chodnoff, Nicki. "Lakewood Cemetery: Man's Hand Complements Nature's Artistry in Minneapolis." *American Cemetery* (May 1992): 18-19; 24-26.

Churchill, Henry W. *Churchill's Guide Through the Albany Rural Cemetery*. Albany, NY, 1857.

Clark, Kenneth. *The Gothic Revival: An Essay in the History of Taste*. London, 1962.

Clarke, Rod. *Carved in Stone: A History of the Barre Granite Industry*. Barre, VT, 1989.

Cleaveland, Nehemiah. *Green-Wood: A Directory for Visitors*. New York, 1857.

———. *Green-Wood Cemetery: A History of the Institution From 1836 to 1864*. New York, 1866.

———. *Green-Wood Illustrated*. New York, 1847.

———. *Hints Concerning Green-Wood: Its Monuments and Improvements*. New York, 1853.

Clegg, Frances. "Problems of Symbolism in Cemetery Monuments." *Journal of Garden History* 4:3 (1984): 307-315.

Colvin, Howard. *Architecture and the After-Life*. New Haven, CT, 1991.

Combs, Diana Williams. *Early Gravestone Art in Georgia and South Carolina*. Athens, GA, 1986.

Connelly, Thomas L. *The Marble Man: Robert E, Lee and His Image in American Society*. New York, 1977.

Corbett, Harvey V. "The Value of Memorial Architecture." *Architectural Forum* 45:6 (1926): 321-324.

Crawford, Sybil F. *Jubilee: The First 150 Years of Mount Holly Cemetery, Little Rock, Arkansas*. Little Rock, AR, 1993.

Craven, Wayne. *Sculpture in America*. New York, 1984.

———. *The Sculptures at Gettysburg*. Gettysburg, PA, 1982.

Creese, Walter L. *The Crowning of the American Landscape: Eight Great Spaces and Their Buildings*. Princeton, NJ, 1985.

Cret, Paul B. "Memorials—Columns, Shafts, Cenotaphs and Tablets." *Architectural Forum* 45.6 (1926): 331-336.

Cronin, Xavier A. "The Cemetery in America—Part 2: The Rural Cemetery Movement." *American Cemetery* (April 1993): 18-19; 26-32.

Crook, J. Mordaunt. *The Greek Revival: Neo-Classical Attitudes in British Architecture, 1760-1870*. London, 1972.

The Crown Hill Cemetery: Past, Present, and Future. Indianapolis, 1988.

Culbertson, Judi and Tom Randall. *Permanent Californians: An Illustrated Guide to the Cemeteries of California*. Chelsea, VT, 1989.

———. *Permanent Londoners: An Illustrated Guide to the Cemeteries of London*. Post Mills, VT, 1991.

———. *Permanent New Yorkers: A Biographical Guide to the Cemeteries of New York*. Chelsea, VT, 1987.

———. *Permanent Parisians: An Illustrated Guide to the Cemeteries of Paris*. Chelsea, VT, 1986.

Cunliffe, Marcus. *George Washington: Man and Monument*. Boston, 1958.

Curl, James Stevens. *A Celebration of Death: An Introduction to Some of the Buildings, Monuments and Settings of Funerary Architecture in the Western European Tradition.* New York, 1980.

_____. "The Design of the Early British Cemeteries." *Journal of Garden History* 4.3 (1984): 223-54.

_____. *The Egyptian Revival.* London, 1982.

_____. *The Victorian Celebration of Death.* Detroit, 1972.

Dansel, Michel. *Au Père Lachaise: Son histoire, ses sécrets, ses promenades.* Paris, 1973.

Darnall, Margaretta J. "The American Cemetery as Picturesque Landscape: Bellefontaine Cemetery, St. Louis." *Winterthur Portfolio: A Journal of American Material Culture* 18.4 (1983): 249-69.

Davis, Stephen. "Empty Eyes, Marble Hands: The Confederate Memorial and the South." *Journal of Popular Culture* 16 (1982): 2-21.

Dearborn, Nathaniel S. *Dearborn's Guide Through Mount Auburn Cemetery.* Boston, 1847 (annual editions published thereafter until 1858).

deBrunhoff, Anne. *Souls in Stone: European Graveyard Sculpture.* New York, 1978.

Deetz, James. *In Small Things Forgotten: The Archaeology of Early American Life.* Garden City, NY, 1977.

Denon, Dominique-Vivant. *Voyage dans la Basse et la Haute Égypte pendant les campagnes du général Bonaparte.* 3 vols. Paris, 1802; rpt. New York, 1973.

de Pouilly, J.N.B. *3 Nouvélle Orleans.* (Original sketchbook, in archives of Historic New Orleans Collection.)

Déscription de l'Égypte; ou, Recueil des observations et des recherches qui ont éte faites en Égypte pendant l'expédition de l'armée francaise, publié par les odres de Sa Majesté, l'empereur Napoléon le Grand. 21 vols. Paris, 1809-1828.

Dickerson, Robert B., Jr. *Final Placement: A Guide to the Deaths, Funerals and Burials of Notable Americans.* Algonac, MI, 1982.

Dillahunty, Albert. *Shiloh National Military Park.* Washington, D.C., 1955.

Dimmick, Lauretta. "Thomas Crawfords's Monument for Amos Binney in Mount Auburn Cemetery, 'A Work of Rare Merit'." *Markers: Journal of the Association for Gravestone Studies* 9 (1992): 160-195.

Doezama, Marianne and June Hargrove. *The Public Monument and Its Audience.* Cleveland, 1977.

Donnell, Edna. "A.J. Davis and the Gothic Revival." *Metropolitan Museum Studies* 5.2 (1936): 183-233.

Douglas, Ann. *The Feminization of American Culture.* New York, 1977.

_____. "Heaven Our Home: Consolation Literature in the Northern United States, 1830-1880." In *Death in America.* Ed. David E. Stannard. Philadelphia, 1975: 49-68.

Downing, Andrew Jackson. "Public Cemeteries and Public Gardens." *The Horticulturist* 4 (1849): 345-51.

Durand, J.N.L. *Précis des lecons d'architecture données à l'Ecole Polytechnique.* Paris, 1802-1805.

_____. *Recueil et paralléle des édifices en tout genre, anciens et modernes.* Paris, 1800.

Early, James. *Romanticism and American Architecture.* New York, 1965.

Eastlake, Charles L. *A History of the Gothic Revival.* London, 1872.

Eckels, Claire Wittler. "The Egyptian Revival in America." *Archaeology* 3 (1950): 164-169.

Ellis, G. Edward. *Sketches of Bunker Hill Battle and Monument.* 2nd ed. Charlestown, MA, 1843.

Ellis, Nancy and Parker Hayden. *Here Lies America: A Collection of Notable Graves.* New York, 1978.

Emerson, Bettie Alder Calhoun. *Historic Southern Monuments: Representative Memorials of the Heroic Dead of the Southern Confederacy.* New York, 1911.

Esdaile, Katherine A. *English Church Monuments, 1510-1840.* London, 1946.

Etlin, Richard. *The Architecture of Death: The Transformation of the Cemetery in Eighteenth-Century Paris.* Cambridge, MA, 1984.

_____. "Landscapes of Eternity: Funerary Architecture and the Cemetery, 1793-1881." *Oppositions* 8 (1977): 14-31

Evans, James Matthew. *The Landscape Architecture of Washington, D.C.: A Comprehensive Guide.* Washington, D.C., 1981.

Everhart, William C. *Vicksburg National Park.* Washington, D.C., 1954.

Farrell, James J. *Inventing the American Way of Death, 1830-1920.* Philadelphia, 1980.

Fenza, Paula J. "Communities of the Dead: Tombstones as a Reflection of Social Organization." *Markers: Journal of the Association for Gravestone Studies* 7 (1989): 136-157.

Firth, Raymond. *Symbols: Public and Private.* Ithaca, NY, 1973.

Fish, Lydia. *The Last Firebase: A Guide to the Vietnam Veterans Memorial.* Shippensburg, PA, 1987.

Fitch, James Marston. *American Building 1: The Historical Forces That Shaped It.* 2nd ed. Boston, 1966.

Flagg, Wilson. *Mount Auburn: Its Scenes, Its Beauties, and Its Lessons.* Boston, 1861.

Forbes, Harriette Merrifield. *Gravestones of Early New England and the Men Who Made Them, 1653-1800.* Boston, 1927. Rpt. Brooklyn, NY, 1989.

_____. "Symbolic Cemetery Gates in New England." *Old Time New England* 24 (1933): 46-58. Rpt. in *Markers: Journal of the Association for Gravestone Studies* 7 (1990): 3-18.

"Forest Lawn: Buffalo's Renowned Gallery of Memories." *American Cemetery* (June 1986): 16-20.

Forest Hills Cemetery: Its Establishment, Progress, Scenery, Monuments, Etc. Roxbury, MA, 1855.

Frazee, John. "The Statue and Monument to Washington." *North American Review* 5 (1835): 350-52.

Freeman, James A. "The Protestant Cemetery in Florence and Anglo American Attitudes Toward Italy." *Markers: Journal of the Association for Gravestone Studies* 10 (1993): 218-42.

French, Stanley. "The Cemetery as Cultural Institution: The Establishment of Mt. Auburn and the 'Rural Cemetery Movement'." *American Quarterly* 26 (1974): 37-59. Rpt. in *Death in America.* Ed. David. E. Stannard. Philadelphia, 1975: 69-91.

Fried, Frederick and Edmund V. Gillon Jr. *New York Civic Sculpture: A Pictorial Guide.* New York, 1976.

Friedlander, Lee. *The American Monument.* New York, 1976.

Fulton, Linda de K. "Memorials of the American Revolution." *Chautauquan* 31 (1900): 365-377.

Gallagher, H. M. Pierce. *Robert Mills, Architect of the Washington Monument, 1781-1855.* New York, 1855.

Gandolfo, Henri A. *Metairie Cemetery: An Historical Memoir.* New Orleans, 1981.

Gayle, Margot. "A Portfolio of Harriette Forbes's Cast-Iron Gates." *Markers: Journal of the Association for Gravestone Studies* 7 (1990): 19-33.

Geist, Christopher D. "Historic Sites and Monuments as Icons." In *Icons of America.* Eds. Ray B. Browne and Marshall Fishwick. Bowling Green, OH, 1978: 57-66.

Gerdts, William H. *American Neo-Classic Sculpture: The Marble Resurrection.* New York, 1973.

Gettysburg: The National Shrine. Rev. ed. Gettysburg, PA, 1975.

Giedion, Sigfried. *Space, Time and Architecture.* Cambridge, 1941.

Gilchrist, Agnes Addison. *William Strickland, Architect and Engineer, 1788-1854.* Enlarged ed. New York, 1969.

Gillon. Edmund V., Jr. *Victorian Cemetery Art.* New York, 1972.

Gittings, Clare. *Death, Burial and the Individual in Early Modern England.* London, 1984.

Gleason, William J. *History of the Cuyahoga County Soldiers' and Sailors' Monument.* Cleveland, 1894.

Goode, James M. *The Outdoor Sculpture of Washington, D.C.: A Comprehensive Historical Guide.* Washington, D.C., 1974.

Gowans, Alan. *Images of American Living: Four Centuries of Architecture and Furniture as Cultural Expression.* Philadelphia, 1964.

Greenough, Horatio. *Letters of Horatio Greenough, American Sculptor.* Ed. Nathalia Wright. Madison, WI, 1972.

Greenwald, Marilyn and Brian Heston. "Woodlawn Cemetery." *Stone in America* (Feb. 1988): 36-43.

Greenwald, Marilyn and Robert Wright. "Metairie Cemetery." *Stone in America* (Aug. 1988): 26-33.

Gurney, Gene. *Arlington National Cemetery.* New York, 1965.

Habenstein, Robert W. and William M. Lamers. *Funeral Customs the World Over.* Rev. ed. Milwaukee, 1963.

_____. *The History of American Funeral Directing.* Rev. ed. Milwaukee, 1962.

Halttunen, Karen. "Death and Mourning in the Victorian Era." *Henry Ford Museum and Greenfield Village Herald* 12 (1984): 124-131.

Hamlin, Talbot E. *Benjamin Henry Latrobe.* New York, 1955.

_____. *Greek Revival Architecture in America.* New York, 1964.

Hampton, William Judson. *Presidential Shrines from Washington to Coolidge.* Boston, 1928.

Hanks, Jacqueline. "Mausoleum Design." *Stone in America* (Nov. 1990): 12-19.

Harris, Neil. *The Artist in American Society: The Formative Years.* New York, 1966.

_____. "The Cemetery Beautiful." In *Passing: The Vision of Death in America.* Ed. Charles O. Jackson. Westport, CT, 1977: 103-111.

Harvey, David. "Monument and Myth." *Annals of the Association of American Geographers* 69 (1979): 362-381.

Harvey, Frederick L. *History of the Washington National Monument and Washington National Monument Society.* Washington, D.C., 1903.

Hatfield, R.G. *The American House-Carpenter.* New York, 1845.

Haviland, John. *Practical Builder's Assistant.* Baltimore, 1830.

Heath, Caroline R. *Four Days in May: Lincoln Returns to Springfield.* Springfield, IL, 1965.

Heinz, Bernard and T. Charles Erickson. "Grove Street Cemetery: The Nation's Oldest Incorporated Burial Ground, Parts 1 & 2." *American Cemetery* (July 1987): 22-26; (Aug. 1987): 35-39.

Hess, Elizabeth. "A Tale of Two Memorials." *Art in America* 71:4 (1983): 121-126.

Hill, J.B. *Basic Elements of Memorial Design.* Evanston, IL, 1967.

Hillairet, Jacques. *Les 200 Cimetières du vieux Paris.* Paris, 1958.

Hillman, Benjamin J. *Monuments to Memories.* Richmond, VA, 1965.

Hills, Chester. *The Builder's Guide.* Hartford, CT, 1834.

Hinkel, John Vincent. *Arlington: Monument to Heroes.* Rev. ed. Englewood Cliffs, NJ, 1970.

Hitchcock, Henry-Russell, Jr. *The Architecture of H. H. Richardson and his Times, 1838-1886.* New York, 1936.

_____. *Architecture: Nineteenth and Twentieth Centuries.* Baltimore, 1971.

Holt, Dean W. *American Military Cemeteries: A Comprehensive Illustrated Guide to the Hallowed Grounds of the United States.* Jefferson, NC, 1991.

Howard, Jerry. "Mount Auburn Cemetery." *Stone in America* (March 1988): 26-34.

Howlett, Catherine M. "The Vietnam Veterans Memorial: Public Art and Politics." *Landscape* 28.2 (1985): 1-9.

Hubbard, William. "A Meaning for Monuments." *The Public Interest* 74 (1984): 17-30.

Huber, Leonard V. *Clasped Hands: Symbolism in New Orleans Cemeteries.* Lafayette, LA, 1982.

_____. et al. *New Orleans Architecture, Vol III: The Cemeteries.* Gretna, LA, 1974.

Hurlburt. D. Scott. "War Memorials." *Stone in America* (June 1985): 38-43.

Jackson, John B. *Discovering the Vernacular Landscape.* New Haven, CT, 1984.

_____. *The Necessity for Ruins and Other Topics.* Amherst, MA, 1980.

_____. "The Vanishing Epitaph: From Monument to Place." *Landscape* 17 (1967): 22-26.

Jackson, Kenneth T. and Camilo José Vergara. *Silent Cities: The Evolution of the American Cemetery.* New York, 1989.

s'Jacob, Henriette. *Idealism and Realism: A Study of Sepulchral Symbolism.* Leiden, 1954.

Janiak, Ann Corcoran and Brian Heston. "Lake View Cemetery." *Stone in America* (July 1988): 28-37.

Jansen, Lee. "Affordable Affluence." *Stone in America* (May 1993): 30-34.

Jansen, Lee and Michael Drummond. "Mount Royal Cemetery." *Stone in America* (March 1992): 20-26.

Jansen, Lee and Brian Heston. "Père Lachaise: City of the Dead." *Stone in America* (Dec. 1992): 42-48.

Jansen, Lee and Anthony J. Sylvestro. "Hollywood Cemetery." *Stone in America* (Jan. 1989): 26-31.

Jansen, Lee and Robert Wachs. "The Lexington Cemetery." *Stone in America* (July 1990): 20-27.

Jansen, Lee and Robert Wright. "Cave Hill Cemetery." *Stone in America* (Dec. 1989): 26-33.

_____. "Crown Hill Cemetery." *Stone in America* (Sept. 1990): 20-27

_____. "Graceland Cemetery." *Stone in America* (April 1991): 24-32.

_____. "Lakewood Cemetery." *Stone in America* (Sept. 1991): 22-27.

_____. "Mountain View Cemetery." *Stone in America* (June 1991): 24-29.

Jarvis, James Jackson. *Art Thoughts*. Cambridge, MA, 1869.

Jeane, D. Gregory. "The Upland South Folk Cemetery Complex: Some Suggestions of Origin." In *Cemeteries and Gravemarkers: Voices of American Culture*. Ed. Richard E. Meyer. Ann Arbor, MI, 1989; rpt. Logan, UT, 1992: 107-136.

Johnson, Edward C., Gail R. Johnson, and Melissa Johnson. "Oak Woods: Chicago." *American Cemetery* (Jan. 1986): 12-16.

Johnson, Gerald W. *Mount Vernon: The Story of A Shrine*. New York, 1953.

Jones, Barbara. *Design for Death*. New York, 1967.

A Journey Through History: Touring Bellefontaine Cemetery. St. Louis, 1983.

Kates, Charles. "Père Lachaise, Parts 1-3." *American Cemetery* (June 1984): 18-24; (July 1984): 29-36; (Aug. 1984): 21-30.

Kean, Robert H. *History of the Graveyard at Monticello*. Charlottesville, VA, 1972.

Kellogg, Augusta W. "Public Memorials to Women." *New England Magazine* (Jan. 1901): 512-31.

Kemp, B. *English Church Monuments*. London, 1980.

Kidney, Walter C. *Allegheny Cemetery: A Romantic Landscape in Pittsburgh*. Pittsburgh, 1990.

_____. *The Architecture of Choice: Eclecticism in America, 1880-1930*. New York, 1974.

Kimball, Fiske. *Thomas Jefferson, Architect and Builder*. Cambridge, MA, 1916.

Koykka, Arthur S. *Project Remember: A National Index of Gravesites of Notable Americans*. Algonac, MI, 1986.

Kurtz, Donna C. and John Boardman. *Greek Burial Customs*. New York, 1971.

Laas, William. *Monuments in Your History*. New York, 1972.

Laborde, Alexandre-Louis-Joseph, Comte de. *Les Monumens de la France*. 2 vols. Paris, 1816.

Laird, Archibald. *Monuments Marking the Graves of the Presidents*. Hanover, MA, 1971.

Lancaster, Clay. "Oriental Forms in American Architecture, 1800-1870." *The Art Bulletin* 29 (1947): 183-193.

Lancaster, R. Kent. "Green Mount: The Introduction of the Rural Cemetery Into Baltimore." *Maryland Historical Magazine* 74.1 (1979): 62-79.

Lanctot, Barbara. *A Walk Through Graceland Cemetery*. Rev. ed. Chicago, 1982.

Landy, Jacob. *The Architecture of Minard Lefever*. New York, 1970.

_____. "The Washington Monument Project in New York." *Journal of the Society of Architectural Historians* 28 (1969): 291-297.

Langley, Batty. *Ancient Architecture Restored and Improved by a Great Variety of Useful Designs, Entirely New, in the Gothic Mode for the Ornamenting of Buildings and Gardens*. London, 1742.

_____. *Gothic Architecture, Improved by Rules and Proportion*. London, 1747.

Latrobe, Benjamin Henry Beneval. *Impressions Respecting New Orleans by Benjamin Henry Beneval Latrobe: Diary & Sketches, 1818-1820*. Ed. Samuel Wilson, Jr. New York, 1951.

Linden, Blanche M. G. "The Willow Tree and Urn Motif." *Markers: Journal of the Association for Gravestone Studies* 1 (1980): 149-156.

Linden-Ward, Blanche. " 'The Fencing Mania': The Rise and Fall of Nineteenth-Century Funerary Enclosures." *Markers: Journal of the Association for Gravestone Studies* 7 (1990): 35-58.

_____. "Nature by Art and Design: The Art and Landscape of Cincinnati's Spring Grove." Documentary Videotape (28.5 min.). Cincinnati, 1987.

_____. "Putting the Past in Place: The Making of Mount Auburn Cemetery." *Proceedings of the Cambridge Historical Society* 44 (1985): 171-96.

_____. "Putting the Past Under Grass: History as Death and Cemetery Commemoration." *Prospects: An Annual of American Cultural Studies* 10 (1985): 279-314.

_____. *Silent City on a Hill: Landscapes of Memory and Boston's Mount Auburn Cemetery*. Columbus, OH, 1989.

_____. "Strange But Genteel Pleasure Grounds: Tourist and Leisure Uses of Nineteenth Century Rural Cemeteries." In *Cemeteries and Gravemarkers: Voices of American Culture*. Ed. Richard E. Meyer. Ann Arbor, MI, 1989; rpt. Logan, UT, 1992: 293-328.

Linden-Ward, Blanche and David C. Sloane. "Spring Grove: The Founding of Cincinnati's Rural Cemetery, 1845-1855." *Queen City Heritage: The Journal of the Cincinnati Historical Society* 43:1 (1985): 17-32.

Linden-Ward, Blanche and Alan Ward. "Spring Grove: The Role of the Rural Cemetery in American Landscape Design." *Landscape Architect* 75:5 (1985): 126-31; 140.

Lindley, Kenneth. *Graves and Epitaphs*. London, 1972.

Litten, Julian. *The English Way of Death: The Common Funeral Since 1450*. London, 1991.

Lockwood, Charles and Marvin Newman. "Green-Wood: Fashionable Cemetery with a View." *Smithsonian* 7:4 (1976): 56-63.

Loth, Calder and Julius Trousdale Sadler, Jr. *The Only Proper Style*. New York, 1975.

Loudon, J.C. *On the Laying Out, Planting, and Managing of Cemeteries, and on the Improvement of Church Yards*. London, 1843.

Lowenthal, David. "The Place of the Past in the American Landscape." In *Geographies of the Mind*. Eds. David Lowenthal and Martyn J. Bowden. New York, 1976.

Ludwig, Allan I. *Graven Images: New England Stonecarving and its Symbols, 1650-1815*. Middletown, CT, 1966.

MacCloskey, Monro. *Hallowed Ground: Our National Cemeteries*. New York, 1968.

Marion, John Francis. *Famous and Curious Cemeteries*. New York, 1977.

Marty, Joseph. *Promenades pittoresques aux cimetière du Père Lachaise*. Paris, 1835.

Marx, Leo. *The Machine in the Garden: Technology and the Pastoral Ideal in America*. New York, 1964.

Masson, Ann M. "Père La Chaise and New Orleans Cemeteries." *Southern Quarterly* 31.2 (1993): 82-97.

May, George S. *Michigan Civil War Monuments*. Detroit, 1965.

Mayo, James M. *War Memorials as Political Landscape: The American Experience and Beyond*. New York, 1988.

McDannell, Colleen. 'The Religious Symbolism of Laurel Hill Cemetery." *The Pennsylvania Magazine of History and Biography* 111.3 (1987): 275-303.

McDannell, Colleen and Bernhard Lang. *Heaven: A History*. New Haven, CT, 1988.

McDowell, Peggy. "J.N.B. de Pouilly and French Sources of Revival Style Design in New Orleans Cemetery Architecture." In *Cemeteries and Gravemarkers: Voices of American Culture*. Ed. Richard E. Meyer. Ann Arbor, MI, 1989; rpt. Logan, UT, 1992: 137-158.

_____. "Martin Milmore's Soldiers and Sailors Monument on the Boston Common: Formulating Conventionalism in Design and Symbolism." *Journal of American Culture* 11.1 (1988): 63-86.

_____. "New Orleans Cemeteries: Architectural Styles and Influences." *Southern Quarterly* 20.1 (1982): 9-27.

McGann, Tom. "Amazing Graceland: Chicago's Historic Burial Ground, Parts 1-2." *American Cemetery* (July 1986): 14-19, 40-42; (Aug. 1986): 16-20.

_____. "Chicago's Rosehill Cemetery, Parts 1-2." *American Cemetery* (June 1988): 18-24; (July 1988): 22-30,

McManners, John. *Death and the Enlightenment: Changing Attitudes to Death Among Christians and Unbelievers in Eighteenth Century France*. Oxford, 1981.

Meller, Hugh. *London Cemeteries: An Illustrated Guide and Gazetteer*. 2nd ed. London, 1985.

Messinger, Ruth E. "Atlanta's Oakland Cemetery." *American Cemetery* (Feb. 1989): 24-25; 36-37; 40-41.

_____. "Crown Hill Cemetery: Pride of Indianapolis." *American Cemetery* (Jan. 1989): 21-25.

_____. "Green-Wood Observes 150th Anniversary." *American Cemetery* (Dec. 1988): 34-38; 53.

_____. "Revisiting Woodlawn Cemetery." *American Cemetery* (March 1989): 18-22.

Meyer, Richard E. *Ethnicity and the American Cemetery*. Bowling Green, OH, 1993.

_____. "Image and Identity in Oregon's Pioneer Cemeteries." In *Sense of Place: American Regional Cultures*. Eds. Barbara Allen and Thomas J. Schlereth. Lexington, KY, 1990: 88-102.

_____. " 'So Witty As to Speak'." In *Cemeteries and Gravemarkers: Voices of American Culture*. Ed. Richard E. Meyer. Ann Arbor, MI, 1989; rpt. Logan, UT, 1992: 1-6.

Miller, J. Jefferson, II. "The Designs for the Washington Monument in Baltimore." *Journal of the Society of Architectural Historians* 23 (1964): 18-28.

Miller, Lillian B. "Paintings, Sculpture, and the National Character, 1815-1860." *Journal of American History* 53 (1967): 696-707.

Mills, Robert. "Essay on Architectural Monuments." *Analectic Magazine* (April 1820): 277-93.

Mitchell, Mary H. *Hollywood Cemetery: The History of a Southern Shrine.* Richmond, VA, 1985.

Mitford, Jessica. *The American Way of Death.* New York, 1963.

Morgan, Keith N. "The Emergence of the American Landscape Professional: John Notman and the Design of Rural Cemeteries." *Journal of Garden History* 4.3 (1984): 269-89.

Morley, John. *Death, Heaven and the Victorians.* Pittsburgh, 1971.

Morrison, Hugh. *Louis Sullivan: Prophet of Modern Architecture.* New York, 1935.

Mount Vernon: An Illustrated Handbook. Mount Vernon Ladies' Association of the Union, 1974.

Mueller, Eileen. *Two Hundred Years of Memorialization.* Evanston, IL, 1976.

Murphy, Buck P. "Victorian Cemetery Art." *Design* 75.2 (1974): 6-9.

"National Cemeteries." *Harper's New Monthly Magazine* (Aug. 1886): 310-22.

Newton, Robert Hale. *Town and Davis.* New York, 1942.

Nishiura, Elizabeth. *American Battle Monuments: A Guide to Military Cemeteries and Monuments Maintained by the American Battle Monuments Commission.* Detroit, 1989.

Norman, L. Aine. *Monuments funeraires.* Paris, 1847.

Notman. John. *Guide to Laurel Hill Cemetery.* Philadelphia, 1844.

O'Donnell, Joseph. *The Paths of Glory: A Guide to the Gravesites of Our Deceased Presidents.* West Bethesda, MD, 1992.

Olson, Peggy Maize. "Gettysburg." *Stone in America* (Nov. 1991): 22-29.

Opt, Susan. "Rock Creek Cemetery." *Stone in America* (Jan. 1988): 14-21.

Palmer, Francis M. "The Tombs of Our Presidents." *Munsey's Magazine* (Nov. 1901): 224-32.

Panofsky, Erwin. *Tomb Sculpture: Four Lectures on Its Changing Aspects from Ancient Egypt to Bernini.* Ed. H.W. Janson. New York, 1964.

Paprocki, Sherry Beck. "Bellefontaine Cemetery." *Stone in America* (Oct. 1988): 30-37.

Penny, Nicholas. *Church Monuments in Romantic England.* New Haven, CT, 1977.

Peters, James Edward. *Arlington National Cemetery: Shrine to America's Heroes.* Kensington, MD, 1986.

Pevsner, Nikolaus. *A History of Building Types.* Princeton, NJ, 1976.

Pevsner, Nikolaus and S. Lang. "The Egyptian Revival." In *Studies in Art, Architecture and Design.* Vol. 1. Ed. Nikolaus Pevsner. New York, 1968: 213-35.

Pickney, Pauline A. *American Figureheads and Their Carvers.* New York, 1940.

Pike, Martha V. "In Memory of: Artifacts Related to Mourning in Nineteenth Century America." In *American Material Culture: The Shape of Things Around Us.* Ed. Edith Mayo. Bowling Green, OH, 1984: 48-65.

Pike, Martha V. and Janice Gray Armstrong. *A Time to Mourn: Expressions of Grief in Nineteenth Century America.* Stony Brook, NY, 1980.

Prospectus of the General Cemetery Company. London, 1830.

Puckle, Bertram S. *Funeral Customs: Their Origin and Development.* London, 1926; rpt. Detroit, 1990.

Pugin, Augustus Welby. *An Apology for the Revival of Christian Architecture in England.* London, 1843.

_____. *The True Principles of Pointed or Christian Architecture.* London, 1853.

Pugin, Augustus Welby and Augustus Charles Pugin. *Examples of Gothic Architecture.* 3 Vols. London, 1850.

Quaglia, Ferdinand. *Les cimitières de Paris: Recueil de plus rémarquables monuments funèbres avec leurs inscriptions.* Paris, n.d.

_____. *Le Père la Chaise; ou, Recueil de dessins au trait, et dans leurs justes proportions, des principaux monuments de ce cimetière, dessinés et lithographiés par M. Quaglia.* Paris, 1835.

Ragon, Michel. *The Space of Death: A Study of Funerary Architecture, Decoration and Urbanism.* Trans. Alan Sheridan. Charlottesville, VA, 1983.

Rainey, Rueben M. "The Memory of War: Reflections on Battlefield Preservation." *Yearbook of Landscape Architecture.* Vol I. New York, 1983: 69-89.

Rauschenberg, Bradford. "A Study of Baroque- and Gothic-Style Gravestones in Davidson County, N.C." *Journal of Early Southern Decorative Arts* 3 (1977): 24-50.

Rayner, Joan. "Pere-Lachaise." *Architectural Review* 86 (1939): 159-162.

Reiff, Daniel D. "The Whitefield Cenotaph: A Rediscovered Work by William Strickland." *Journal of the Society of Architectural Historians* 33.1 (1974): 48-60.

Remes, Naomi R. "The Rural Cemetery." *Nineteenth Century* 5.4 (1979): 52-55.

Rheims, Maurice. *The Flowering of Art Nouveau.* New York, 1966.

Richardson, James B., III and Ronald S. Carlisle. "The Archaeological Significance of the Mausoleums in the Allegheny and Homewood Cemeteries of Pittsburgh." *Markers: Journal of the Association for Gravestone Studies* 1 (1980): 156-65.

Ridlen, Susanne S. "Funerary Art in the 1890s: A Reflection of Culture." *Pioneer America Society Transactions* 6 (1983): 27-35.

Roe, Alfred Seeyle. *Monuments, Tablets and Other Memorials Erected in Massachusetts to Commemorate the Services of Her Sons in the War of the Rebellion, 1861-1865.* Boston, 1910.

Rooney, Pat and Brian Heston. "Green-Wood Cemetery." *Stone in America* (Nov. 1987): 32-39.

Rooney, Pat and Kris Robbins. "Forest Lawn Cemetery." *Stone in America* (Aug. 1987): 22-31.

Roos, Frank J., Jr. "The Egyptian Style: Notes on Early American Taste." *Magazine of Art* 33 (1940): 218-23.

Roth, Leland M. *The Architecture of McKim, Mead, and White, 1870-1920: A Building List.* New York, 1978.

_____. *A Monograph of the Works of McKim, Mead, and White, 1879-1915.* New York, 1973.

Rotundo, Barbara. "Mount Auburn Cemetery: A Proper Boston Institution." *Harvard Library Bulletin* 22.3 (1974): 268-79.

_____. "Mount Auburn: Fortunate Coincidence and an Ideal Solution." *Journal of Garden History* 4:3 (1984): 255-267.

_____. "The Rural Cemetery Movement." *Essex Institute Historical Collections* 109 (1973): 231-240.

Ruby, Jay. "Portraying the Dead." *Omega: Journal of Death and Dying* 19:1 (1988-89): 1-20.

Sanata, Lawrence. "Monument Design and Architecture." *Stone in America* (Dec. 1984): 34-39.

Saum, Lewis. "Death in the Popular Mind of Pre-Civil War America." In *Death in America.* Ed. David E. Stannard. Philadelphia, 1975: 30-48.

Schlereth, Thomas J. *Artifacts and the American Past.* Nashville, TN, 1980.

_____. *Cultural History and Material Culture: Everyday Life, Landscapes, Museums.* Ann Arbor, MI, 1990; rpt. Charlottesville, VA, 1992.

_____. *Victorian America: Transformations in Everyday Life, 1876-1915.* New York, 1991.

Schofield, Mary Peale. *Landmark Architecture of Cleveland.* Pittsburgh, 1976.

Schorsch, Anita. "A Key to the Kingdom: The Iconography of a Mourning Picture." *Winterthur Portfolio: A Journal of American Material Culture* 14.1 (1979): 41-71.

_____. *Mourning Becomes America: Mourning Art in the New Nation.* Clinton, NJ, 1975.

Schroeder, Fred E. H. *Outlaw Aesthetics: Arts and the Public Mind.* Bowling Green, OH, 1977.

Schuyler, David. "The Evolution of the Anglo-American Rural Cemetery: Landscape Architecture as Social and Cultural History." *Journal of Garden History* 4.3 (1984): 291-304.

_____. *The New Urban Landscape: The Redefinition of City Form in Nineteenth Century America.* Baltimore, 1986.

Schwartz, Barry. "The Social Context of Commemoration: A Study in Collective Memory." *Social Forces* 61 (1982): 374-402.

Scott, Grant F. "Meditations in Black: The Vietnam Veterans Memorial." *Journal of American Culture* 13.3 (1990): 37-40.

Scott, Jonathan. *Piranesi*. New York, 1975.

Scully, Vincent. *The Earth, The Temple, and The Gods: Greek Sacred Architecture*. New York, 1969.

Seta, Alessandro Della. *Religion and Art*. London, 1914.

Sharf, Frederic A. "The Garden Cemetery and American Sculpture: Mount Auburn." *Art Quarterly* 34.2 (1961): 80-88.

Siegel, Stewart. "Hollywood Cemetery: The Final Home of Three Presidents." *American Cemetery* (Nov. 1987): 18-22; 36-38.

Simon, Donald. "Green-Wood Cemetery and the American Park Movement." In *Essays on the History of New York City: A Memorial to Sydney Pomerantz*. Ed. Irving Yellowitz. Port Washington, NY, 1978: 61-77.

Slater, James A. *The Colonial Burying Grounds of Eastern Connecticut and the Men Who Made Them*. Hamden, CT, 1987.

Sloane, David Charles. *The Last Great Necessity: Cemeteries in American History*. Baltimore, 1991.

Smith, Deborah A. "'Safe in the Arms of Jesus': Consolation on Delaware Children's Gravestones." *Markers: Journal of the Association for Gravestone Studies* 4 (1987): 85-106.

Smith, John Jay. *Designs for Monuments and Mural Tablets Adapted to Rural Cemeteries and Church Yards*. Philadelphia, 1846.

_____. *Guide to Laurel Hill Cemetery, Near Philadelphia*. Philadelphia, 1844.

Smith, R.A. *Smith's Illustrated Guide to and through Laurel Hill Cemetery*. Philadelphia, 1852.

Snyder, Ellen Marie. "Innocents in a Worldly World: Victorian Children's Gravemarkers." In *Cemeteries and Gravemarkers: Voices of American Culture*. Ed. Richard E. Meyer. Ann Arbor, MI, 1989; rpt. Logan, UT, 1992: 11-29.

Spargo, John. *The Bennington Battle Monument*. Rutland, VT, 1925.

Stanley, John Francis. "The Exedra in Memorial Design." In *Memorial Art, Ancient and Modern*. Ed. Harry Bliss. Buffalo, 1912.

Stannard, David E. "Calm Dwellings: The Brief Sentimental Age of the Rural Cemetery." *American Heritage* 30 (1979): 42-46; 54-60.

Stilgoe, John R. *Common Landscapes of America, 1580 to 1845*. New Haven, 1982.

Stillman, Damie. "Death Defied and Honor Upheld: The Mausoleum in Neo-Classical England." *The Art Quarterly* (New Series) 1 (1978): 175-213.

Strickland, William. *Tomb of Washington at Mount Vernon*. Philadelphia, 1840.

Stubben, J. "Municipal Memorials." *Municipal Affairs* 3 (1899): 724-731.

Sullivan, James R. *Chickamauga and Chattanooga Battlefields*. Washington, D.C., 1956.

Svanevik, Michael and Shirley Burgett. *Pillars of the Past: A Guide to Cypress Lawn Memorial Park, Colma, California*. San Francisco, 1992.

Tashjian, Dickran and Ann. *Memorials for Children of Change: The Art of Early New England Stonecarving*. Middletown, CT, 1974.

Thane, Elswyth. *Mount Vernon Is Ours: The Story of Its Preservation*. New York, 1966.

_____. *Mount Vernon: The Legacy. The Story of Its Preservation and Care Since 1885*. Philadelphia, 1967.

Thomas, Samuel W. *Cave Hill Cemetery: A Pictorial Guide and Its History*. Louisville, KY, 1985.

Toynbee, J.M C. *Death and Burial in the Roman World*. New York, 1971.

Trask, Deborah. *Life How Short, Eternity How Long: Gravestone Carving and Carvers in Nova Scotia*. Halifax, NS, 1978.

Trudell, Clyde F. *Colonial Yorktown*. New York, 1971.

Twombly, Robert. *Louis Sullivan: His Life and Work*. New York, 1986.

van Brunt, Henry. *Architecture and Society: Selected Essays of Henry van Brunt*. Ed. W.A. Coles. Cambridge, MA, 1969.

_____. "The Washington Monument." *The American Art Review* 1 (1880): 7-9.

Vogel, Frederick G. "Green-Wood Cemetery, Parts 1-4." *American Cemetery* (Jan. 1985): 16-20, 39; (Feb. 1985): 21-28, 32; (March 1985): 31-43; (April 1985): 22-26.

_____. "Proud and Historic Crown Hill Cemetery." *American Cemetery* (May 1991): 22-23; 30-37.

Voller, Jack G. "The Textuality of Death: Notes on the Reading of Cemeteries." *Journal of American Culture* 14.4 (1991): 1-9.

Von Blum, Paul. *The Critical Vision: A History of Social and Political Art in the U.S.* Boston, 1982.

Wallace, Robert. "The Elegies and Enigmas of Romantic Père Lachaise." *Smithsonian* 9.11 (1978): 108-117.

Warner, W. Lloyd. *The Living and the Dead: A Study of the Symbolic Life of Americans.* New Haven, CT, 1959.

Warren, George Washington. *The History of the Bunker Hill Monument Association.* Boston, 1877.

Watters, David H. *'With Bodilie Eyes': Eschatological Themes in Puritan Literature and Gravestone Art.* Ann Arbor, MI, 1981.

Weaver, Lawrence. *Memorials and Monuments.* New York, 1915.

Weil, Tom. *The Cemetery Book.* New York, 1992.

Welch, Richard F. *Memento Mori: The Gravestones of Early Long Island, 1680-1810.* Syosset, NY, 1983.

Wheaton, Henry. "Egyptian Antiquities." *North American Review* 30.65 (Oct. 1829): 361-388.

Wheildon, William W. *Memoir of Solomon Willard, Architect and Superintendent of the Bunker Hill Monument.* Boston, 1865.

Whitlock, Susan Opt. "Columnar Monuments." *Stone in America* (Sept. 1986): 12-17.

_____. "Exedrae and Screens." *Stone in America* (Oct. 1986): 40-45.

_____. "Mausoleums." *Stone in America* (Dec. 1986): 18-25.

_____. "Obelisks." *Stone in America* (May 1986): 34-39.

_____. "The Sarcophagus." *Stone in America* (Nov. 1986): 18-23.

Whittemore, Frances Davis. *George Washington in Sculpture.* Boston, 1933.

Whittick, Arnold. *History of Cemetery Sculpture.* London, 1938.

Widener, Ralph W. *Confederate Monuments: Symbols of the South and the War Between the States.* Washington, D.C., 1982.

Willard, Solomon. *Plans and Sections of the Obelisk of Bunker's Hill, with Experiments Made in Quarrying the Granite.* Boston, 1843.

Wills, Garry. *Lincoln at Gettysburg: The Words That Remade America.* New York, 1992.

Wilson, Jane B. *The Very Quiet Baltimoreans: A Guide to the Historic Cemeteries and Burial Sites of Baltimore.* Shippensburg, PA, 1991.

Wilson, Richard G. *McKim, Mead, and White.* New York, 1983.

Wilson, Samuel, Jr. and Leonard Huber. *The St. Louis Cemeteries of New Orleans.* New Orleans, 1968.

Wilson, William H. *The City Beautiful Movement.* Baltimore, 1989.

Wilton-Ely, John. *The Mind and Art of Giovanni Battista Piranesi.* London, 1978.

Winberry, John J. "Symbols in the Landscape: The Confederate Memorial." *Pioneer America Transactions, 1982*: 9-15.

_____. " 'Lest We Forget': The Confederate Monument and the Southern Townscape." *Southeastern Geographer* 23:2 (1983): 107-21.

Wright, Robert A. "Calvary Cemetery: Milwaukee's Landmark Burial Ground." *American Cemetery* (Jan. 1987): 13-17.

_____. "Forest Home Cemetery." *Stone in America* (Jan. 1991): 14-21.

_____. "Great Entrance Gates." *Stone in America* (Dec. 1988): 26-31.

_____. "Mausoleum Montage." *Stone in America* (April 1988): 28-33.

_____. "Oak Woods Cemetery." *Stone in America* (May 1989): 26-33.

_____. "Poems in Stone: The Tombs of Louis Henri Sullivan." *Markers: Journal of the Association for Gravestone Studies* 5 (1988): 168-208.

_____. "Spring Grove Cemetery, Parts 1-2." *American Cemetery* (Sept. 1987): 18-23; (Oct. 1987): 32-34, 69-70.

Young, Melvin. *Where They Lie.* Lanham, MD, 1991.

Zanger, Jules. "Mt. Auburn Cemetery: The Silent Suburb." *Landscape* 24.2 (1980): 23-28.

Zelinsky, Wilbur. *Nation Into State: The Shifting Symbolic Foundations of American Nationalism.* Chapel Hill, NC, 1988.

_____. "O Say, Can You See?: Nationalist Emblems in the Landscape." *Winterthur Portfolio: A Journal of American Material Culture* 19.4 (1984): 77-86.

Zubowsky, John. "Monumental American Obelisks: Centennial Vistas." *The Art Bulletin* 58.4 (1976): 574-581.

Index